I0820205

HOME BARTENDING MASTERY

This book is dedicated to Anika Poitier, who dragged me, sometimes kicking and screaming, into the life I've always wanted.

And to my mom, Graciela Pari Di Monriva, without whom I wouldn't be here in both obvious and non-obvious ways.

Quarto.com

First Published in 2025 by The Harvard Common Press,
an imprint of The Quarto Group,
100 Cummings Center, Suite 265-D, Beverly, MA 01915, USA.
T (978) 282-9590 F (978) 283-2742

29 28 27 26 25 1 2 3 4 5

ISBN: 978-0-7603-9378-9

Digital edition published in 2025
eISBN: 978-0-7603-9379-6

Library of Congress Cataloging-in-Publication Data available.

Photographer: David Koung Peng. IG: @davidkoungphoto
www.davidkoungphotography.com

Prop stylist: Jaclyn Kershek

Photo assistant: Yihu Jin

Design and Page Layout: Studio quarante douze (Montréal)
Cover Image: David Koung Peng, www.davidkoungphotography.com
Photography: David Koung Peng, www.davidkoungphotography.com
Illustration: Studio quarante douze (Montréal)

Printed in China

HOME BARTENDING MASTERY

Iconic Cocktails to Build Skills and Drink Better

Leandro Pari Di Monriva

HARVARD
COMMON
PRESS

Contents

Introduction: Master the Classics

I found my way to bartending the way so many others have, it's become a cliché. It was a means to an end. I needed my days free to audition for acting jobs and whatever job I could do at night had to be lucrative so I could afford my rent on as few days of work as possible. The answer came in the form of a recommendation for a barbacking job at a Hollywood nightclub from a guy I was working with on the set of a commercial. In the moment, I thought I was solving a practical problem; it never occurred to me that the opportunity that would materialize would change the course of my life.

When I left my hometown to move to Los Angeles and pursue a career as an actor, my mom's fear was: What would happen if my big (and embarrassing) dreams of stardom weren't realized? And I assured her, that whatever happened, I was sure that following this path would lead me to what I was meant to do, acting or otherwise. Boy was I right.

Over the course of my eighteen-year career behind the bar, I have been asked time and again for my advice on making drinks. Although I never realistically thought I'd get the opportunity to write a book, I have done my best to answer those questions, and it was those questions, added to my absolute passion for cocktails and the bartenders that made them, that led me to start a YouTube channel with my longtime friend and collaborator Marius Haugan. At the time of its creation, The Educated Barfly was one of only a handful of channels dedicated to the craft of the cocktail, and one of only two headed up by a professional bartender. Since the beginning of that journey, the videos have amassed more than 60 million views over 11,000 videos. The mission has always been simple: to share my passion and knowledge for cocktails and help people make and drink better drinks. We wanted to cut through the misinformation on the internet and be one of the best resources out there for incredible cocktail recipes and, more importantly, the correct techniques for making them. Because, as you will find as you go through the pages of this book, it's the technique that really matters. As of this writing, seven years after we began, I can proudly say that I think we have succeeded in our mission.

The purpose of this cocktail guide doesn't lie in the recipes it contains; recipes are a dime a dozen—good or bad, everybody has one. This book endeavors to help you understand cocktails at a fundamental level, to answer the why as well as the how. Because once you know why you're doing what you're doing, everything else falls into place.

You'll be empowered to not only make your own recipes but really understand recipes when you look at them—and you'll be armed with professional techniques to make the best drinks possible.

I approach making videos the way I would start to train a new barback who was interested in becoming a bartender, and so the first series I made was called *Master the Classics*. Just like learning to walk before you run, to be great at cocktails you need to understand the classic recipes and why they work. Those recipes are all based on a handful of cocktail templates created during the Golden Age of Cocktails (roughly 1850 to 1919). Every cocktail in existence is based on one of these recipes, and I wanted this book to reflect that. First, you'll get the classic recipe, then some modern riffs made by bartenders I admire, and, of course, a few originals that I came up with. With those examples it's my hope you'll understand the inner workings of the cocktail and that they'll inspire in you the love for a great drink.

amomille

CHAPTER 1

Understanding Spirits

The first step in understanding cocktails is to understand their main ingredients, and those would be the spirits you'll use to create them. Although it's most important to understand the flavors of each spirit, as you will be pairing them with modifiers to make balanced and delicious drinks, it also helps to know about their production process and even their history. This will help you with an appreciation for the spirit itself, the culture it came from, and more importantly, the nuances between different styles, which are often regional. To this end, I'd like to give you a short overview of each spirit you'll find used to make the cocktails in this book. It isn't ALL the information, but it is enough to get you started. I implore all of you to read more deeply into spirits' history and production—not only is it fascinating stuff, but it can only help you on your cocktail journey.

WHISKEY

At its heart, whiskey is any distilled spirit made from a fermented grain mash and usually aged in wooden barrels that are typically oak. This broad definition fits a massive category of spirits with a host of different styles, each with their own unique characteristics. Some of these styles adhere to strict rules and geographic locations and some do not.

As a note, given that whiskey is spelled differently based on its country of origin, I will be observing the convention of spelling it correctly for each region. As a rule, if you're referring to it in Canada, Japan, or Scotland it is spelled whisky without the "e." The United States and Ireland, on the other hand, spell the word *whiskey* with the "e." In this book, when referring to whiskey in general, I will use the "e."

RYE

There are a couple of different stories surrounding the history of rye whiskey. Some say it was introduced to North America by Dutch farmers in the Colony of New Amsterdam (what is now the southern tip of Manhattan) in the 1640s, while others say it emerged in Pennsylvania in the 1750s. Whatever the truth, we do know that it is America's very first whiskey. The two major styles that emerged are the Monongahela style from Pennsylvania and Maryland-style rye.

Over time it has been eclipsed by the popularity of its younger brother bourbon. Rye has a very distinctive yeast-like flavor and natural spiciness that can take some getting used to, whereas bourbon is more naturally sweet due to its higher corn content. But rye has been making a strong comeback in recent years.

To be able to be labeled as "straight rye whiskey": It has to be made from at least 51 percent rye, be distilled to no higher than 160 proof (80 percent alcohol by volume [ABV]), aged for at least two years in new charred oak barrels, be put into barrels at no higher than 125 proof (62.5 percent ABV), contain no additives, and be bottled at no less than 80 proof (40 percent ABV).

BOURBON

Most sources say that bourbon as a singular style emerged in the 1780s in the part of the United States we now know as Kentucky. As time moved on and people pushed the frontier south, distilling moved with them, and they started using corn as a base ingredient for spirits. The whiskey coming out of that region was likely labeled bourbon as a tip of the hat to the French royal family in honor of their support during the Revolution. The name stuck, and the same term began to be applied to whiskey being made in neighboring areas as well.

Bourbon follows all of the same rules as rye whiskey. To be able to be labeled as "straight bourbon whiskey": It has to be made from at least 51 percent corn, be distilled to no higher than 160 proof (80 percent alcohol by volume [ABV]), aged for at least two years in new charred oak barrels, be put into barrels at no higher than 125 proof (62.5 percent ABV), contain no additives, and be bottled at no less than 80 proof (40 percent ABV).

CANADIAN

Whisky production started a little later in Canada than in the United States. It was English brewer and entrepreneur John Molson who is credited with introducing whisky to Canada in 1799. That said, several groups such as Scottish, Irish, and American immigrants were also responsible for the introduction and evolution of whisky in Canada. And it was the Dutch and Germans who are typically credited with the addition of rye grain to the mash to help improve flavor. Although there was a lot of distilling going on, the first legal distillery was opened in 1832.

Canadian whisky must be made with cereal grains grown in Canada such as corn, wheat, rye, and barley, and must be aged in wooden barrels no larger than 700 liters for a minimum of three years. The spirit must be at least 40 percent ABV and must say "Product of Canada" on the label. That's about it.

SCOTCH

Probably the best-known category of whisky, Scotch has a long history and has been made as early as the fifteenth century. Scotch starts as three simple ingredients: malted barley, spring water, and yeast. Scotch must be produced in Scotland and aged in oak casks for a minimum of three years. If an age statement is included on the bottle, it must reflect the age of the youngest whisky in the bottle and it must be bottled at no less than 80 proof (40 percent ABV). Most Scotch is sold as blended, which means the whisky is a blend of single malt and grain whisky from different distilleries. But one of the most popular is single malt whisky, which means the Scotch must be made entirely of malted barley, be distilled using a pot still, and, of course, be aged for at least three years.

IRISH

Like Scotch, Irish whiskey has a long history dating back to the early fifteenth century. The first documented mention of whiskey in Ireland dates to 1405. This whiskey must be produced in the Republic of Ireland, be made from barley (both malted and unmalted) and other cereal grains, and be distilled to no higher than 94.8 percent alcohol. It must be bottled at no less than 80 proof (40 percent ABV), and the use of plain caramel coloring is permitted.

JAPANESE

The Japanese have been making whisky for over a hundred years and make what is considered some of the finest whiskies in the world. Japanese whisky started with a young chemist named Masataka Taketsuru who travelled to Scotland in the early 1900s to learn the art of whisky making. While there, he apprenticed at distilleries such as Longmorn and Hazelburn. In 1920 he returned to Japan where he would eventually co-found Yamazaki distillery.

Japanese whisky must be made entirely at a Japanese distillery, it must contain malted grain—either barley, rye, or wheat—and may contain other cereal grains, must use water from Japan, and must be aged at least three years.

GIN

The story of gin starts with the Dutch and a spirit they made called Genever. Genever is a spirit originally made from malted wine and juniper berries distilled in a pot still. It has been made since the Middle Ages and was used as a medicinal tonic. By the 1600s, it became popular as a recreational drink with not only the Dutch but also Belgians, the French, and Germans. And it was only a little later in this century that English troops brought it back to England where it became popular during the Thiry Years' War. It is believed that soldiers drank it to bolster their courage and began referring to it first as "Gen," which eventually became "gin." Over time the distillation process changed, and the base spirit became one made of grain. Little by little, modern gin was born.

Gin doesn't have a lot of fixed rules to be classified as gin, only that it must be made from a neutral spirit that comes from a natural source such as grains, grapes, or potatoes, and that juniper berry is its primary flavoring. With that said, modern gin breaks down into four major styles: London Dry, Plymouth, Old Tom, and New World.

LONDON DRY

London Dry must be made from a neutral spirit of agricultural origin and distilled to a minimum of 96 percent ABV. All botanicals added must be natural and added during the distillation process. Finally, water is added to bring the proof of the spirit down. Although sweetener is allowed, only 0.1 percent can be added per liter. Although there are no strict rules for which botanicals are added outside of juniper, you'll usually find coriander, orris root, angelica root, citrus peel, licorice root, and cassia bark in its makeup.

PLYMOUTH

Plymouth gin can be confusing because although it is a style of gin, it is also a brand of gin, and that particular brand is the only one making Plymouth gin nowadays—although there were other distilleries making it in the past. Plymouth gin can only be produced in Plymouth, England, must be distilled to at least 37.5 percent ABV, and is pot distilled. The botanicals you'll find are very similar to London Dry, but this gin is a bit earthier and a touch sweeter. Common botanicals are: orris root, angelica root, lemon peel, cardamom, sweet orange, and coriander.

OLD TOM

Old Tom emerged during the eighteenth and early nineteenth centuries when gin was a rougher spirit due to less attention to the rectification of base spirits. More congeners (chemicals created in the fermentation process that contribute to the smell and taste of spirits) were left in less purified spirits, making them harder to drink. Thus, people started sweetening the gin with various botanicals and sugar to make it more palatable. Nowadays, Old Tom is made to a higher standard but follows the same principles of sweetening or sometimes even barrel aging the gin.

NEW WORLD

Although gin took a backseat to vodka beginning in the 1940s, in modern culture—and due to a massive resurgence in classic cocktails and cocktail culture in general—it has come to the forefront once again. We have been in a massive distillation boom over the past fifteen years, which means we have a LOT of new gins on the market. New World is a broad term that covers this new style of gin; it often emphasizes its other botanicals over juniper and is usually made with botanicals native to the area where it's produced. These are the crazy, anything-goes gins we see popping up all over the world, and it is this style of gin that is pushing the envelope in the category.

VODKA

The history of distillation in the East is murky at best, and a lot of this information has been lost to time. We do know that the Russians have been making vodka since the 1490s, and the Polish were home distilling their version of vodka since the early 1400s. Vodka began its introduction to the West when some major distillers were forced to flee in the wake of the Bolshevik Revolution.

Vodka can be made from any natural source, such as potato, grain, sugar beet, or fruit. It is typically distilled by column distillation, which will produce higher proof and purer distillates. The rules for vodka are that it must be distilled to 190 proof (95 percent ABV) in the United States and 192 proof (96 percent ABV) in Europe. It typically isn't aged in wood and is often charcoal filtered to further remove any color or character. In the past, the definition of vodka was that it must be treated so as to have no distinct flavor, aroma, character, taste, or color, which is a little ridiculous given that vodkas distilled from different sources have different characteristics no matter how much you try to remove them. In 2020, the definition was changed to remove that requirement.

TEQUILA/ MEZCAL

Although Mexicans have been making agave-based fermented alcoholic beverages since around 250 AD, it was the Spanish who introduced distillation to Mexico in the sixteenth century. It was then that people began to test distillation of the agave plant, and it was those tests that first introduced mezcal, and later tequila. There is a saying that, "All tequila is mezcal but all mezcal is not tequila." Both spirits are made from the heart of the agave plant, which is called the piña. Technically tequila is a specialized expression of mezcal, so what're the differences between these two spirits?

MEZCAL

The word *mezcal* comes from the words *metl* and *ixcalli,* which translates to "oven-cooked agave." Unlike tequila, mezcal can be made from any species of agave plant, although there are some more common than others. The most common species used are *espandin, tobala, tepeztate, tobaziche,* and *arroqueno.* Mezcal must be made in Mexico and can only be made in nine Mexican states: Oaxaca, Guerrero, Puebla, Michoacan, Tamaulipas, Guanajuato, Zacatecas, Durango, and San Luis Potosi. It must fall between 70 proof (35 percent ABV) and 110 proof (55 percent ABV).

TEQUILA

Tequila emerged in the 1600s, and commercial production began by the mid-1750s. Tequila was given a designation to set it apart from any other agave spirits in 1902. There are two types of tequila: "Mixto" and tequila made from 100 percent agave. Mixto is so named because it is a mix of distillates. Up to 49 percent of the distillate can be from a non-agave sugar source such as sugar beets or cane sugar. This type of tequila is of lower quality, and I don't recommend it. The other style, which is labelled 100 percent puro de agave, has a set of rules and regulations that must be adhered to, also known as the NOM (Norma Oficiale Mexicana), and is regulated by the CRT (Consejo Regulatdor de Tequila).

To be labelled as 100 percent agave tequila it must only be made from the Blue Weber variety of agave, be aged between fourteen and twenty-one days, be made in one of five Mexican states (Guanajuato, Jalisco, Nayarit, Tamaulipas, or Michoacan), and be bottled between 70 proof (35 percent ABV) and 110 proof (55 percent ABV). These tequilas fall into one of five categories:

BLANCO This style is tequila that has been aged for less than two months.

JOVEN This means "young" in Spanish. This is a blend of blanco tequila and either reposado or añejo.

REPOSADO Tequila that has been aged for over two months but less than a year.

AÑEJO Aged in oak barrels for at least a year but under three.

EXTRA AÑEJO Aged for more than three years.

BRANDY

Surprisingly, brandy is an often overlooked and very misunderstood spirit. Partially because the category has been eclipsed by Cognac, a very specialized form of brandy, and also because it is a vast category with many different expressions—most of which are a bit niche. To put it simply, any spirit distilled from fermented fruit is considered brandy. The most common expressions, Cognac and spirits labelled simply as "brandy," are made from fermented grapes (i.e., wine), but spirits made from *any* fruit is brandy.

The word *brandy* comes from the Dutch word *brandewijn*, which translates to "burnt wine" in English. It has been made in Europe since the early fourteenth century when its first uses were medicinal (of course) and was first commercialized by the Dutch in the seventeenth century. In America, colonists would make a form of brandy called apple-jack by burying a cask of apple cider in the earth in wintertime. As the ground froze, the water in the cider would freeze as the apple fermented, leaving a core of apple-based alcohol at its center. Then in 1780, a Scottish immigrant named William Laird began to distill his own apple brandy and sell it. Apple brandy was the first distilled spirit native to the United States.

Here are the most common forms of brandy, some of which you'll find in cocktails in this book, and some of which you won't but should know about anyway. Let's start with the most famous:

COGNAC Cognac is a brandy made with white grapes solely from the Cognac region of France. Some varietals typically used are Ugni Blanc, Folle Blanc, or Collombard. It must be distilled twice in a copper pot still, must be at least 40 percent alcohol by volume, and cannot be made with wine that contains added sulfites. Aging requirements depend on three classifications of Cognac:

VS (VERY SPECIAL)
Aged for at least two years

VSOP (VERY SUPERIOR OLD PALE)
Aged for at least four years

XO (EXTRA OLD)
Aged for at least ten years

ARMAGNAC This is a brandy from the Armagnac region of France in the southwest. This expression is distilled once and, again, aging is dependent on classification:

VS (VERY SPECIAL)
Aged for at least one year

VSOP (VERY SUPERIOR OLD PALE)
Aged for at least four years

XO (EXTRA OLD)
Aged for at least six years

HORS D'AGE
Aged for at least ten years

CALVADOS This is an apple brandy that must be made in the Normandy region of France from apples grown in the same region. The cider must be left to ferment at room temperature for at least twenty-one days, must be aged for a minimum of two years in French oak barrels, and must be bottled at 40 percent ABV.

APPLEJACK An American apple brandy first distilled in 1780 and America's first distilled spirit. There are several distillers making applejack today, with Laird's being the first and most prominent in production.

BRANDY Anything labeled simply "brandy" is made with grapes without rules surrounding its production. In the past, this was seen as low quality or only fit for cooking, but that perception is beginning to change with more and more companies making high quality brandy.

EAU DE VIE This is a colorless style brandy made from many different fruits. It usually clocks in at 40 to 60 percent ABV, so it can be a bit higher in proof than other types and is typically unaged.

RUM

Rum is a spirit made in just about every country in the world. It emerged in the early 1700s when enslaved people working on Caribbean plantations discovered that molasses, the byproduct of sugar production, would ferment. In this way they turned what was once seen as waste into a commodity that could be traded. The molasses was sent up to the colonies in America and distilled into rum.

Rum doesn't have a lot of fancy rules and regulations around its production, only that it must be made out of sugarcane, or its byproducts, and because of this it's a vast and incredibly diverse category. The lack of rules surrounding it also makes it very hard to summarize neatly, so there is a lot of confusion around rum and it's this very fact that has hampered its mass popularity. Terms like "light" and "dark," or categorizing by region just don't convey the diversity of the spirit, because no one region is married to a specific style the way a spirit like whiskey is. The best way to categorize rum is by using the Gargano classification system, which goes by raw material and production method. Here's how rum breaks down:

PURE SINGLE RUM Made from molasses and distilled in a pot still. Rums made with a pot still are going to be much more flavorful than those made with a column still. It is less refined and contains many more chemicals such as esters, aldehydes, and methanol, which contribute to a more pronounced flavor profile. Some common flavors are underripe banana, tropical fruit, and burnt sugar. Flavors will vary from region to region.

PURE SINGLE AGRICOLE RUM Made from fresh sugarcane juice and distilled in a pot still. Agricole rum, usually spelled rhum, has a bright, vegetal flavor, which is much more different than its molasses counterpart. Along with this very distinct flavor, it can also contain the same funky tropical fruits you'll find in molasses-based rums.

SINGLE BLENDED A blend of pot and column still rums. Flavors run the gamut here, as this is a massive category that can be any number of combinations, and of course they'll vary region to region. What you are likely to get in these rums is oak character from barrel aging, as well as spices such as cinnamon and nutmeg, along with tropical fruit notes such as banana, pineapple, or mango.

TRADITIONAL RUM Distilled in a traditional column still. Column stills distill and redistill in one cycle, so the spirits are stronger and more neutral than those made with a pot still. This is not only a great way of getting rid of impurities, but also a great way to distill flavors out of the final product. Again, many rums are made this way including Cuban and Cuban-style rums. It's helpful to note that unlike other spirits categories, rums that are clear aren't necessarily unaged. Oftentimes, producers will age a rum in wood for a couple years then run the rum through a charcoal filter to remove the color.

MODERN RUM Distilled in a modern multi-column still. These rums use a multi-column system of continuous distillation that allows for unprecedented control over the final product and is more cost effective as well. These rums tend to be lighter and sharper in flavor than those made with a pot still.

AMARO, APERITIFS, AND FORTIFIED WINES

Amaro, aperitifs, and fortified wines were almost unheard of in American bars fifteen years ago. Many bars had a dusty bottle of vermouth sitting with the other spirits, not even in the fridge where it belongs. Every now and again the bartender would dust it off to make a Martini. Much has changed in the years following, thank god. With the cocktail explosion of the late 1990s and early 2000s, not only can you find all of these spirits, but they are also ubiquitous in any cocktail bar worth its salt. Amaro is becoming so popular that it has whole bars dedicated to cocktails made with it, and you know what? Those bars are incredibly popular. We've finally done it—we've made the American drinker just as sophisticated as they were in the nineteenth century! We've finally gotten back what we lost during prohibition!

AMARO

Amaro, which is the Italian word for "bitter," is a bittersweet Italian liqueur commonly drunk as an after-dinner digestif (a drink consumed to aid digestion). It is made by macerating a mixture of herbs, spices, citrus peels, and barks with neutral spirits, wine, or a combination of the two. It is then mixed with sugar syrup and allowed to age in wooden casks or glass bottles. Amari (the plural of amaro) tend to be lower proof, around 16 to 20 percent ABV, but some, such as Fernet Branca, run as high as 40 percent. Although modern amari has over two hundred years of history, with many brands tracing their creation to the mid-nineteenth century, its origins go back as far as the ancient Romans who created bitter tonics for medicinal purposes. Amari are highly regional, and although there are no hard and fast rules that govern how they're created, they do break down into a few different styles such as Fernet (higher in alcohol and flavored with mint, saffron, chamomile, and myrr), Carciofo (made with artichoke), Rhabarbaro (made with rhubarb), Tartuffo (made with black truffle) China (primarily flavored with cinchona bark) and Alpine (flavored with herbs and flowers of the Alpine region).

APERITIFS

Aperitif liqueurs are very similar to amari and even have many of the same ingredients. It is also a bittersweet liqueur, but where amaro is dark, bitter, and used to help digest food, aperitifs are light, bright red, and used to help stimulate the appetite before a meal. They tend to be dry and not too sweet with pronounced bitterness, although, like amari, they run the spectrum between sweeter and drier with some variation in bitterness as well. Some examples of aperitifs are Campari, Aperol, and Select.

VERMOUTH

There are a whole host of fortified wines used for cocktails, but the most common is vermouth. Fortified wines are a class of alcoholic beverage that have a base of wine with a spirit (typically brandy) added to it to bring more dimension as well as a bit more shelf life. Vermouth comes in three main varieties: dry, sweet, and blanc. Back in the days of yore, dry and sweet were known as French and Italian respectively. Nowadays, companies in both France and Italy make all the varieties of vermouth. Vermouth is made by macerating a white wine or mistelle base with all manner of botanicals, then fortifying it with spirits—usually brandy or another grape-based distillate. All recipes are proprietary, so each vermouth has many of its own characteristics, although it is generally agreed that true vermouth must contain wormwood.

Sweet vermouth is typically dark in color from the addition of caramel coloring; it's noticeably sweet and has notes of warming spices.

Dry will be lighter in both color and on the palate. It will be more herbaceous and drier with a sharpness on the palate.

Blanc is a bit lighter than dry vermouth. It is also clear and herbaceous and very floral with pronounced citrus. This option is best used in cocktails with more delicate flavors, as robust flavors can overrun it very easily.

OTHER AROMATIZED WINES

Throughout this book you'll find I call for a few other aromatized wines for use in cocktails. These products are made much in the same way as vermouth but have very different flavor profiles. They are sometimes used in place of vermouth to add more complexity to a drink.

COCCHI AMERICANO Sweet with a pronounced bitterness, it has flavors of grapefruit and lemon along with wormwood and gentian root. It has a medium-long finish with a snap of cinchona bark, which gives it a quinine forward aftertaste.

LILLET BLANC Lillet is a blend of Bordeaux wines macerated not only with herbs but also with citrus peels and fruit liqueur. Its original formula contained quinine, but the current one does not.

QUINAQUINA This is a style of aromatized wine named after its main flavoring ingredient, cinchona bark, which gives it a pronounced quinine flavor

BITTERS

If you've been in a bar or around cocktails at all, you've probably heard of bitters. Bitters are an extremely concentrated infusion of herbs, spices, barks, citrus peels, and other botanicals in alcohol or vegetable glycerin. Today, bitters are almost exclusively used for cocktails, but historically they evolved for medicinal use to cure non-serious ailments such as stomach cramping and hangovers. Bitter herb macerations have been used in homeopathy since the ancient Egyptians, but they started being applied medicinally to spirits in the 1700s in England. Shortly thereafter, they hopped the pond to the United States where they became incredibly popular in the mid 1800s, and it was around this time that they also made their way into cocktails.

The best way to understand bitters and how to use them is to look at them like seasonings for your cocktail—not unlike how you use salt, pepper, and other spices to season your food. There are those bitters that are meant to add a new flavor and balance to your drink, such as aromatic bitters. These are very spice-dominant in flavor, hitting you over the head with clove, cinnamon, nutmeg, and notes of chocolate, coffee, and dark fruit. And there are bitters meant to amplify other flavors in your drink. These are going to be more delicate in flavor and a little easier to work with. Bitters can be challenging to incorporate: Just the right amount can elevate your drink to a new level, whereas too much can muddy flavors and ruin a drink. The best way to approach using bitters, especially if you're using them in your own creations, is to add them dash by dash, tasting along the way until you hit the money spot. You'll know when you hit the nail on the head, and you'll know if you've added too much.

We are in a bitters boom at the moment. Since the reintroduction of serious cocktails and many bartenders looking back into history for inspiration, bitters are having a moment. Where fifteen years ago you'd be hard pressed to find any bitters at your local liquor store, we're now flush with bitters made in every conceivable combination in every conceivable flavor. Lucky for you guys, you'll only need three different bitters to execute the vast majority of the cocktails in this book. My first time out I wanted to keep things simple. That's doesn't mean there aren't a few bottles of different bitters throughout the recipes, only that you won't be inundated with having to buy a vast number of bottles. If you like to experiment and want to add to your bitters collection, go for it, but the three that follow are the classics that should always be stocked in any home bar.

ANGOSTURA BITTERS By far the most recognizable of all bitters, it basically comes standard with any bar on the planet. These are the default aromatic bitters used in the industry. If a recipe calls for "bitters" without specifying which kind, its calling for Angostura.

PEYCHAUD'S BITTERS Developed by New Orleans pharmacist Antoine Amedee Peychaud in the mid-1800s, this style of bitters is known as Creole bitters and is most famously found in the Sazerac.

ORANGE BITTERS This is a style of bitters that was impossible to find in the early 2000s and was largely brought back by spirits writer and bartender Gary Reagan when he couldn't find any to execute historic recipes. The orange bitters I use is a mix of Reagan's bitters made with Seville oranges and Fee Brothers Orange Bitters, which has a more neutral orange flavor.

STAINLESS
STEEL

CHAPTER 2

Tools of the Trade

It doesn't matter if you're a star bartender or just starting out, great cocktails require great tools. And not just the physical tools you use to build each drink—you need to think about everything from ice to syrups to glassware to technique. These are the building blocks of drinks—and equate to at least 90 percent of how your drinks will be perceived—so how you execute them is important. In this section we'll go over all of the basics, from actual tangible tools and styles of ice, to syrups and how to make it all work with professional technique. I implore you, no matter whether you make tons of cocktails or very few, please don't cheap out on your tools. Buy yourself professional-grade tools that will last you many years. There are a lot of tools out there, some you need and some you definitely don't. I've decided to list what you need to make the cocktails in this book—and no more. As I say to all the barbacks I've trained to bartend over the years: It's a lot of info but it ain't rocket science. Once you learn to attend to these details, every cocktail you execute from any recipe will be chef's kiss.

BEHIND THE BAR

COCKTAIL SHAKING TINS

There are two different varieties of shaker tins: the two piece and the three piece. A two-piece shaking set consists of a 28-ounce (828 ml) grand tin and 18-ounce (532 ml) mini grand tin. This is the shaking set you mostly see behind professional bars, especially in North America. When the two tins are fitted together properly, they create a lock that allows you to shake the drink. When you're done shaking, you must slap the side of the tins to unlock them. Once you get the hang of them, they are simple to use and easy to clean. These are my preference.

The three-piece set is also called a cobbler shaker. It was invented in 1884 by a guy named Eduard Hauck as an improvement on the two-piece set. It consists of a main cocktail tin, a top with built in strainer, and a small cap to cover the strainer while you shake. You have seen these shakers if you've ever shopped for bar equipment in a Sur La Table or Crate & Barrel. Somehow this style of shaker has become the default for non-professional home bartenders in North America. It is also the style of shaker preferred by professionals in Europe and Japan. This strainer has two fatal flaws though: firstly, the built-in strainer doesn't work well, so every cocktail should be double strained through a fine strainer—but the biggest flaw is in its design. The three pieces of this shaker usually nest together, and when you shake a cocktail, you create a cold vacuum of air inside the tins. It is common for this vacuum to seal the pieces together and make it next to impossible to get back open. You may as well go bury it in your yard as a time capsule for future generations because you're not getting that tin open any time soon.

JIGGER

The jigger is the next most important piece of equipment. Measuring the volume of your ingredients is of the utmost importance, especially if you're new to cocktails or just starting out. Jiggers come in a variety of sizes and shapes and can be found in various measurement standards from ounces to milliliters to centiliters. So, there's a jigger to suit you no matter what standard you adhere to or where you are in the world. Typically, jiggers are two sided with two different measurements on either side, although many companies make jiggers that have several measurements on each side, making it easier to measure cocktails in a couple steps, and replacing the need for several jiggers to make one cocktail.

HAWTHORNE STRAINER

The Hawthorne strainer is a flat metal disc with a handle and metal coil affixed on its outside edge; professional ones also have stabilizing prongs that help it fit on the rim of a cocktail shaking tin and a small tab of metal protruding from the top. The coil rolls forward as you put it on, allowing it to fit snugly inside the cocktail shaker. When straining, you press the tab of metal with your index finger, pushing the strainer down, which retracts the coil allowing it to block ice and debris as you pour.

FINE STRAINER

Handheld fine strainers that are made for cocktailing usually have a large basket allowing it to strain larger volumes. Hawthorne strainers are notoriously bad at blocking all of the debris you may have in your drink, such as shredded ice and mint as well as pieces of muddled fruit. It's a good idea to have an extra strainer in place to get all the stuff the first strainer didn't. I double strain all of my shaken cocktails, and even a few stirred ones to make sure I don't get excess ice chips and other debris in my drink, ensuring a nice, elegant look.

JULEP STRAINER

A julep strainer is a large metal perforated disc with a handle; it looks like a big metal spoon and it's used to strain stirred cocktails. It's a traditional piece of equipment but one I don't deem completely necessary, as what it does can easily be done with a Hawthorne strainer. Essentially, it's a simpler style strainer used to block large pieces of ice and designed to fit a standard mixing glass.

MIXING GLASS

Mixing glasses are elegant 17-ounce (500 ml) vessels used to stir cocktails. Traditionally, they're made from glass or crystal (if you want to get fancy) but can be made from metal or even ceramics.

WEIGHTED BAR SPOON

Bar spoons are long and skinny with a twisted body and small bowl. They come in various sizes, but the most common (and useful) ones are between 12 inches (30 cm) and 15 inches (38 cm) long. Weighted spoons have, as the name implies, a small weight that helps you rotate the spoon around the ice for proper stirring. There are many different styles of spoons. Some have weights, muddlers, strainers, and forks on the ends of them. I recommend a weighted spoon and a spoon with a muddling top to help make Old Fashioneds a cinch.

Y-PEELER

The Y-Peeler is exactly what it sounds like, a peeler in a Y shape. This is the best peeler to use—I can't tell you how hard it is to get good peels using a straight potato peeler. There are several options for these peelers, and a few companies make them with removable blades so you can buy refills and always have a sharp peeler. Making sure your peeler blades are sharp is incredibly important—there's nothing more dangerous than a dull blade.

GLASSWARE

Glassware is an area of cocktail making many people neglect, but it is of utmost importance to getting a great result. Glassware not only determines the look of your drink, but also how the drinker will interact with it. When you serve a cocktail for someone, you get one shot at forming a good impression—fail this, and that impression will stay with the person you served long after they finish the drink you made them. How a cocktail sits in the glass and how it's presented depends greatly on how many ounces it can hold. The end game of using proper glassware for the drinks you serve is to enhance the cocktail experience; the size, shape, thickness, curve, and material of each glass has an impact on the result. For example, many men refuse to drink cocktails out of stemmed cocktail glassware, insisting on drinking every drink on the rocks. Put a Manhattan on the rocks and you're likely adding too much water to the drink over time, leading to a cocktail that tastes like water flavored with a Manhattan. Also, the shape of some glasses is made to concentrate the aroma of a cocktail or spirit to enhance the experience through smell.

Glassware is also a way to express your creativity in cocktail making—there are a vast number of choices within any given style. What you should watch out for is the volume of the glassware you choose; this will determine everything about your cocktail from the way it sits in the glass to the size, amount, and style of ice. It directly affects the overall result of the drink and how it comes across. You must remember that people drink with their eyes first—your cocktail should be beautiful and functional, and there's nothing worse than a tiny cocktail swimming in an oversize glass or vice versa.

DOUBLE OLD FASHIONED/ROCKS

The double old fashioned is a high-capacity rocks glass, usually around 10 to 15 ounces (296 to 444 ml) in volume. It can be in a bucket shape or taper into a V from top to bottom. These glasses are for drinks made on the rocks: drinks in a short glass with ice that benefit from the dilution over time. The types of ice in this glass are usually rock ice if using a single cube, or small cubes of ice such as Kold-Draft.

NEAT/SINGLE ROCKS

These glasses are the smaller version of the double old fashioned or rocks glass. They are typically used to serve people spirits neat (without ice), scaffa cocktails (cocktails without ice served at room temp), and traditionally the Sazerac (see page 55). These glasses range from 6 to 8 ounces (140 to 240 ml).

FOOTED ROCKS GLASS

The footed rocks glass is my go-to for the Sazerac. Most people put their Sazerac in a neat glass while others use a coupe. For me, the footed rocks glass is the way to go, as it is the best of both worlds. It is essentially a neat glass with a wide stem and a wide base. It's an elegant addition to your collection and makes Sazeracs or Mini Old Fashioneds look fantastic.

COUPE

It is said that the coupe was invented in seventeenth-century England by a Benedictine monk and became popular as a Champagne glass in eighteenth-century France. There is a popular rumor that the glass was modeled after the breast of Marie Antoinette, and while this is hard to disprove, it probably isn't true. Either way, while the coupe was a popular Champagne glass in the 1700s, today, it is the cocktail glass of choice when serving cocktails up—without ice—and in a stemmed glass. These drinks tend to not need any more dilution and so are served up. It's got a short, wide bowl and usually has a capacity of 6 to 8 ounces (180 to 240 ml). Coupes also add a bit of elegance to the overall presentation of your cocktail and are widely preferred over the more iconic cocktail glass shape. The cocktails in this book are all made for the 6-ounce version.

COCKTAIL GLASS

This is the official name of the V-shaped martini glass that has become the undisputed icon depicting not just Martinis but also cocktails in general on every neon sign from LA to Tokyo. I like to use these glasses, as they are elegant and nice looking. Some companies make versions that are monstrously big, so avoid anything over 8 ounces (240 ml). Like coupes, these will be anywhere from 5 to 8 ounces (140 to 240 ml).

HIGHBALL GLASS/ COLLINS GLASS

People like to stick the highball and Collins glass together, but to me they're two different glasses. Both are long, skinny tumblers made to serve drinks long—that is, drinks that are lengthened with some form of modifier (usually sparkling) such as soda water, tonic, or soda pop. Where they differ is in volume and shape: The highball will be shorter, squatter, and hold anywhere from 9 to 10 ounces (230 to 300 ml), whereas the Collins is taller, skinnier, and has a 12-ounce (360 ml) volume. The distinction is important because a highball needs less modifier than a Collins does, so serving a highball in a 12-ounce (360 ml) glass often overdilutes the drink.

SYRUPS, CORDIALS, AND MODIFIERS

In their most rudimentary form, cocktails are made up of either spirit, sweetener, and bitters, or spirit, citrus, and sugar. So, syrups and cordials play a massive part in the proper balancing of a good drink. Most of the drinks in this book are simple affairs that don't take a ton of weird ingredients. You won't be rushing off to specialty stores (or ordering online) to obtain the ingredients for each drink in this book; in fact, most of the ingredients you'll need can usually be found in a well-stocked fridge and pantry. That said, there are a few syrups you'll need to make to execute these drinks well. Unless otherwise noted, syrups last two weeks and must be refrigerated.

SIMPLE SYRUP

As stated in the name of this syrup, it is indeed the simplest and the one called for in most recipes. Simple syrup is just the combination of any kind of sugar and water in a one-to-one ratio. Typically, for cocktails you'll want to use refined white sugar. For my money this sugar is what makes a syrup with neutral sweetness. It adds sucrose and nothing else, so it's used to make other ingredients sweet without competing with its flavors. However, if you'd like to add other flavors to a drink, such as adding a molasses note to a Daiquiri, you can up your simple syrup game and use a different sugar such as demerara or turbinado. Also, if you're being as accurate as possible, and you should be, using a scale and making syrups by weight is the best way to do it. Different sugars have different density, and so getting the right ratio is difficult if measuring by volume.

MAKES 2 CUPS (470 ML)

Ingredients

250 grams	**Water**
250 grams	**Granulated sugar**

Preparation

In a small saucepan, heat the water over medium heat until hot but not simmering. (You don't want the sugar to burn.) Remove from the heat and add the sugar, stirring slowly until fully dissolved. Once cool, strain into a bottle and label.

RICH SIMPLE SYRUP

Rich simple syrup is just simple syrup, but this time in a two-to-one ratio. The benefit of using rich simple syrup is that it has a much longer shelf life. It can last almost indefinitely in the fridge. The downside is that you'll have to revamp your cocktail to accommodate the rich syrup: Typically, you'll cut down the volume of the sugar used in the drink, and in some cases, you may need to increase the volume of citrus. Thus, keep that in mind while using this syrup. And just to dispel any confusion, all of the recipes in this book are formulated with a typical one-to-one ratio simple syrup.

MAKES 2 ½ CUPS (588 ML)

Ingredients

250 grams	**Water**
500 grams	**Granulated sugar**

Preparation

In a small saucepan, heat the water over medium heat until hot but not simmering. Remove from the heat and add the sugar, stirring slowly until fully dissolved. Once cool, strain into a bottle and store in the fridge, indefinitely.

HONEY SYRUP

This is one of two syrups I make that I don't make by weight. The reason is that I want to add just enough water to thin out the honey so that I am able to combine it in cocktails but not mute its level of sweetness too much. If you add honey straight from the jar into your shaker, it won't properly combine into the cocktail. The reason for this is that honey seizes up when it gets cold—when it hits the ice in your tin it'll turn hard, like amber. In my humble opinion, though, if you don't add enough honey, it has a hard time coming through in cocktails. The nuances of its flavor are run over by the citrus in the drink, and you lose all of its savory-sweet qualities. I make my honey syrup in a three-to-one ratio to preserve these nuances, and although honey is sweeter than sugar, this method works well and balances better for whatever reason.

Keep in mind that not all honey is created equal. Honey flavor will change from region to region because the bees of different regions pollinate different flowers. I like to use either wildflower or clover honey in my cocktails, so opt for those if you can find them.

MAKES 1 ⅓ CUPS (313 ML)

Ingredients

⅓ cup (79 ml)	**Warm water**
1 cup (235 ml)	**Honey**

Preparation

In a small saucepan, heat the water over medium heat, or if you have an electric kettle, heat it up to 150°F to 170°F (66°C to 77°C). Place the honey in a small bowl, add the water, and stir. It'll take a little time to combine, but just continue to stir until all the water has combined and the honey takes on a thinner quality. Once cool, strain into a bottle and label.

GINGER SYRUP

This syrup used to be a real pain to make, one that required a masticating juicer and the time-consuming peeling of ginger—until I found Jeffery Morgenthaler's hack for making this syrup. All credit goes to him; he's got the recipe on his blog, and it's my go-to method for making ginger syrup.

MAKES 2 CUPS (470 ML)

Ingredients

1 cup (235 ml)	**Water**
1 cup (125 g)	**Rough-cut fresh ginger** (peel on)
1 cup (200 g)	**Granulated sugar**

Preparation

In a small saucepan or electric kettle, heat up the water to 170°F (77°C). In a blender, add the hot water, ginger, and sugar. Blend on high until everything is blended up well and the sugar is dissolved—it'll look like a liquid mash. Strain through a nut milk bag to remove the ginger's fibers and extract the syrup. Bottle and label.

RASPBERRY SYRUP

Raspberry syrup isn't used in a ton of recipes, but I do use it in a few. It's so good and I love playing with it. It's versatile and can be cut into many cocktails, from a Margarita to a Daiquiri. You can use this template as an all-purpose berry syrup recipe—it works well with blackberries and strawberries as well.

MAKES 2 CUPS (470 ML)

Ingredients

2 cups (470 ml)	**Simple Syrup** (page 28), **warm**
300 grams	**Raspberries, rinsed and lightly crushed**
¼ teaspoon	**Citric acid**

Preparation

In a container with a lid, add the crushed raspberries and the simple syrup. Place in the fridge and allow to sit at least 24 hours. You'll notice the sugar leaching out the raspberry juice, making the syrup reddish.

Into a bowl, strain the syrup through a fine-mesh strainer, crushing the solids with a muddler or by hand to extract as much juice as possible. You may want to add a nut milk bag or tea towel to the strainer and strain it again to get rid of any remaining solids (see Note). Add the citric acid and stir until fully mixed. (You can forgo the citric acid—the syrup works without it—but it does give a really nice vibrant kick to the raspberry flavor and acts as a preservative so you can slightly lengthen its life. I highly recommend it.)

Note

You may be tempted to discard the raspberry solids after making the syrup, but I love to try and mitigate waste where I can, and with just a little more effort, you can make it into delicious fruit leather for garnishing or just eating.

Preheat the oven to no more than 200°F (93°C), but if you can get it down to 150°F (66°C) that would be amazing. (If you have a gas stove, utilizing the pilot light will suffice.) To a blender, add the raspberry solids with ¼ cup of simple syrup and blend into a puree. Line a baking sheet with parchment paper and pour the puree onto the baking sheet. With the back of a spoon, spread the puree into as even a coat as you can. Pop into the oven for 6 to 8 hours, until it has bonded together into fruit leather. Remove from the oven, peel away from the parchment, and enjoy!

ORGEAT

Orgeat is a syrup made from almonds that's commonly used in cocktails. It has a long history dating back to sixth-century Europe (and the Middle East). Originally, it was made from barley—the word *orgeat* is a French word that translates to "barley water"—and was typically used as a fever remedy. Over time, almond oil was added as a flavoring element, and over even more time, it evolved into the semi-sweet almond-based syrup we know today. Although you won't find orgeat in tons of recipes, it's commonly used in tropical and tiki drinks, as well as several of my favorite classic cocktails, so it's definitely worth knowing how to make. It's a great syrup to play with in your own cocktails if you're looking to add a little nuttiness, and of course it's a great option to use in lieu of simple syrup.

There are several ways to make orgeat, which take a little bit of elbow grease, and I think they're worth it. Taking extra time to make something well always benefits your cocktails in the end and will ensure that your drinks are always the talk of the party. Or at least your house.

MAKES 2 CUPS (470 ML)

For the Almond Milk

1 cup (140 g) **Blanched almonds**
2 cups (470 ml) **Warm water**

For the Orgeat

2 cups (470 ml) **Almond milk**
400 grams **Granulated sugar**
½ ounce (15 ml) **Cognac**
½ ounce (15 ml) **Amaretto**
¼ teaspoon **Orange flower water**

Preparation

Make the almond milk: In a small skillet, toast the almonds over medium heat. Place them in a Vitamix or blender with the warm water. Blend on high until the almonds are thoroughly pulverized. Place the mixture into a nut bag and strain the liquid into a jar or other container. Discard the solids.

Make the orgeat: In a medium saucepan, add the almond milk over low heat. Once it's steaming but not simmering, remove from the heat and add the sugar; stir until fully combined. Once cooled, add the Cognac, amaretto, and orange flower water and refrigerate for up to three weeks.

MORGENTHALER'S LIME CORDIAL

For my money, Oregon-based bartender Jeff Morgenthaler is quickly earning the title of the West Coast godfather of cocktails. The man is a treasure trove of information all wrapped up in a non-pretentious package. He concocted this cordial to replace the infamous Rose's Lime Cordial, an old-school syrup used in classic cocktails. Rose's was invented by the Scottish owner of a shipyard named Lauchlan Rose in 1867, who patented a process for preserving lime juice without alcohol. He achieved massive success selling his cordial to the British Royal Navy, who used limes to prevent scurvy. Before long, it caught on in popularity beyond sailors. Today, Coca-Cola owns it, and it's produced with high fructose corn syrup, which has no place in today's cocktail culture. Morgenthaler saw a need for a similar product made with more natural ingredients, and his recipe is . . . chef's kiss!

MAKES 2¼ CUPS (530 ML)

Ingredients

250 grams	**Granulated sugar**
8 ounces (240 ml)	**Hot water**
1½ ounces (45 ml)	**Fresh lime juice**
8 grams	**Freshly grated lime peel**
25 grams	**Citric acid**

Preparation

In a blender, combine the sugar, hot water, lime juice, lime peel, and citric acid and blend on medium speed for 30 seconds. Run the ingredients through a fine-mesh strainer to get rid of the solids. Bottle and refrigerate for up to three weeks.

STRAWBERRY LEMON BALM SYRUP

This is a specialty syrup I created while bartending at Cole's French Dip in Downtown Los Angeles for my Strawberry Fields Old Fashioned (page 60). At the time, I was looking for a way to make an Old Fashioned more summery, and the particular summer this drink came around, I had a lot of lemon balm growing in my yard and wanted to use it. The resulting cocktail was a smash hit that became a fixture on the regular menu.

MAKES 2½ CUPS (588 ML)

Ingredients

2 cups (420 g)	**Demerara sugar**
1 cup (235 ml)	**Filtered water**
16 ounces (454 g)	**Strawberries**
1	**Lemon, zested**
1 large bunch	**Lemon balm leaves and stems**

Preparation

In a small saucepan, combine the sugar and water over low heat and stir until the sugar is fully dissolved. Pour into a large non-reactive container, then add the strawberries, lemon zest, and lemon balm. No need to worry if the syrup is still warm; lemon balm is typically used for tea, and we're steeping it to release its flavor. Cover and let stand for 24 hours at room temperature, then place in the refrigerator and allow to steep another 24 hours. When done, strain the mixture through a cheese cloth or nut milk bag into a sterilized container. It will last about a month in the fridge.

ARABICA COFFEE BEAN VERMOUTH

This idea came about while testing different ways to get coffee flavor into a cocktail without utilizing coffee. I had this idea that I could pair the botanicals in vermouth with a more subtle coffee undertone, and this was the result. It worked beautifully and resulted in a drink that's one of my favorites to this day.

MAKES 1½ CUPS (353 ML)

Ingredients

¼ cup (28 g)	**Whole arabica coffee beans**
About 1½ cups (353 ml)	**Carpano Antica sweet vermouth**

Preparation

In a non-reactive container, combine the coffee beans and the sweet vermouth. Allow to infuse for 90 minutes. Store in the refrigerator for up to 3 months.

GARNISHES

Although garnishes are ornamental fixtures of your cocktail and play a critical role in how someone perceives your drink, the best garnishes are also functional as well. At their best, they impart aroma to a drink, which adds another layer of flavor, complementing the drink without throwing the other ingredients off balance. Your sense of smell is a critical part of your sense of taste and is closely linked to your perception of flavor. This gives you an opportunity to create another dimension in your cocktails. Garnishes are made from all manner of bar materials, and as time moves on, the garnishes get more and more inventive and complex. But for the sake of this book—teaching you a targeted group of cocktails—let's stick with the most commonly used.

CITRUS

Citrus is the most dominant garnish and used in many ways, from peels to wedges to wheels. Most every bar will use lime and lemon wedges to grace the lip of their drinks, but the most effective way is to use their peels and zest the oils over a cocktail. This imparts the oils from the peel, adding a nice pop of citrus without any of the acids of the juice. The only time I use a citrus wedge is when I feel that a cocktail might reasonably benefit from an added pop of citrus juice. If you put a wedge on a drink, nine out of ten people will squeeze the juice into their drink. If your drink will be thrown off balance with more citrus, use a wheel.

PEELS

Proper peeling of citrus requires practice and is a bit of an art. You don't want too thin a peel, or you won't be able to zest oils onto your drink, and if your peel is too thick, you run the risk of imparting bitterness into your drink from the pith. When peeling, use a sharp Y-peeler; using a potato peeler is extremely difficult and dangerous to your fingertips. Grasp the peeler in your dominant hand and extend your index finger over the back of the blade. This will help you control the peeler so it doesn't slip. In the other hand, grasp the fruit and tuck your fingertips behind it. Dig the peeler a little way into the skin and pull down in one steady motion. Don't wag the blade back and forth, as it'll give you a wavy peel (if you have to move the blade to actually cut the skin, the blade is dull, and a dull blade is a dangerous one). Once the peel is the desired length, flick your wrist in a semi-circle to make a nice clean cut at the bottom.

When zesting over the cocktail, hold the peel with both hands, resting the sides of the peel against your fingertips, peel-side out over your drink. Then slowly close your fingers, bending the peel, and watch as oil shoots onto your drink. It's important to note that you don't want to hold your peel too close to the drink—keep it three inches over the drink so the oils peacefully rest on the surface of the cocktail.

WEDGES

Cutting wedges is the easiest garnish to make: You simply cut a lime in half, then cut along the line of pith to cut the half into a wedge, and cut the wedge again from the top down to make a smaller wedge. Depending on the size, each lime will give you four or eight wedges.

MINT

Mint is another garnish used in a ton of cocktails—you'll see a fair amount of it in the recipes of this book. Its leaves are muddled into a cocktail to add mint essence, such as in a Mojito (see page 164), and a bouquet is used to ornament the top of cocktails as well as impart a mint essence.

It's helpful to note that mint can wilt very quickly, so it's imperative to prepare it the correct way. Once you're ready to use your mint, the first step is to make mint sprigs. To do this, take each individual mint spring and strip away any bottom leaves, leaving only the top ones. Reserve the leaves for use in drinks. Then shock the mint by dunking it into an ice water bath headfirst. (The stems don't need to be shocked.) Leave them in the water for at least 5 minutes. Afterward, pat them dry, fill a glass or other vessel with room temp water, and put the mint in it. This should perk up your mint so your cocktails don't have wilted leaves, because honestly there's no worse garnish than sad looking mint.

MARASCHINO CHERRIES

These are the least functional and my least favorite garnish for a drink. You'll find cherries in various drinks from the Old Fashioned to the Manhattan to the Cobbler. Most cherries used to make drinks will be found in jars bathing in their own syrup. It's best to find a quality brand such as Luxardo or Toschi. Whatever you do, avoid the neon red or green cherries found in dive bars!

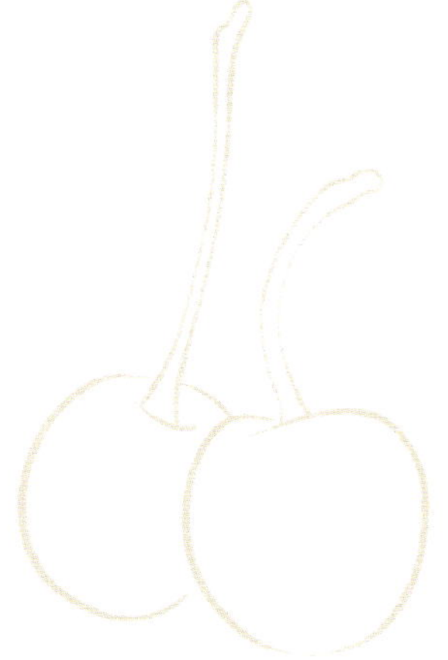

PROPER ICE

Ice is the most debated and argued over ingredient in cocktails, so many people skimp on ice, which is nothing short of criminal. If you think about it, ice makes up the other fifty percent of your cocktail (and I'd argue the most important fifty percent). The shape, size, and temperature of your ice will greatly determine how your cocktails come out. So, what does ice do in your drink? Ice's main function is to chill and dilute: The dilution proofs down your cocktail (reduces the alcohol by volume or ABV), and the chill is greatly responsible for making your drinks taste nice—aside from some notable exceptions, there's nothing worse than a warm drink. The shape and size of your ice is also important because the more surface area your ice takes up in your drink, the more dilution you'll have, determining whether your drink is right on point or overdiluted. And lastly, it's better to use clear ice—not only is it more beautiful, but it is also denser, as it lacks the air pockets and trapped gasses prevalent in cloudy ice. Nowadays, you have a ton of options for getting perfectly clear cocktail ice; most major cities have ice companies dedicating themselves specifically to bars and cocktails, but even if you don't, there are many companies that offer shipping. With these options, you'll have no problem getting the ice you need. With that said, I still like to make my own ice at home and cut it custom. Some might consider it a little overboard, but I love having complete control over how my cocktail sits in the glass and is presented.

There are four major types of ice that you'll use to make the vast majority of cocktails. These are the styles and shapes you'll find in every cocktail bar, and they are all used differently. When attempting to make your own cocktails, it's imperative to consider which type of ice you'll use to achieve the desired effect.

ROCK ICE

This is the style you'll find in many Old Fashioneds and on-the-rocks drinks. It is a single cube designed to fit snugly in a double old fashioned glass. They range in size from 1¾ × 1 × 2½ inches (4.4 × 2.9 × 6.3 cm) to 2 × 2 × 3 inches (5 × 5 × 7.6 cm). Rock ice is preferable in any cocktail that sits on the rocks because its size and clarity control the rate of dilution in your drink.

CUBES

You'll encounter a lot of different iterations of cubed ice. By far the most used across bars is the dreaded hotel pan ice—I've included a section below about why you should avoid it at all costs. If you step into a proper cocktail bar—meaning, one that pays attention to the details of a drink—nine times out of ten, they're using Kold-Draft ice. Kold-Draft cubes are produced by the namesake machine, and it produces a 1 × 1 × 1¼-inch (2.5 × 2.5 × 3.2 cm) cube. These cubes have no indent like hotel pan ice does, so it is denser and shreds less in a cocktail shaker when shaking. Although a Kold-Draft machine isn't feasible for your home, most ice companies have one and sell these cubes. At home, I usually cut these cubes by hand from a larger block of ice.

SPEAR

This style of ice is a column made to fit into a Collins or highball glass. It ranges in size a bit, starting at 1¼ × 1¼ × 5 inches (3.2 × 3.2 × 12.7 cm). These are completely optional, as you can also just fill a Collins with cubes, but it looks very elegant and I love using them. This type of ice acts a lot like rock ice in your drinks, in that it'll control dilution, which is convenient for these drinks that are lengthened with soda water, tonic, or soda pop, which adds dilution to the whole.

PEBBLE/CRUSHED

Even though I grouped them together, pebble and crushed ice aren't the same thing. Pebble ice is made by a machine that produces small, mostly uniform pellets of ice. This is my preferred style of ice, and there are several machines on the market intended for home use that make this type of ice. You can also get a pretty good bag of this at fast food restaurants for around five bucks. This ice is for drinks that require rapid chilling and a little more dilution over time.

HOTEL PAN ICE

If it makes sense telling you about all the ice you *should* use in your drinks, it also makes sense to tell you about what you should avoid if you can. Hotel pan ice refers to the type of ice you'd find in a hotel lobby ice machine or a big warehouse store. It is ice that is frozen in an ice mold that drops into the body of the machine. They are small pieces of ice with an indent on one side, which compromises the integrity of the ice. It melts quickly and you should avoid it at all costs.

TECHNIQUE

This section is what the heart of this book is all about. Any time I begin to train someone to make cocktails, I always drill home the importance of knowing proper technique. Any fool can go to the bookstore and purchase a cookbook from a celebrity chef and try to execute recipes. But what you make is most definitely not going to be the same as if you ordered the dish at one of their restaurants. Because what separates you from the restaurant chefs is technique. They have techniques that you don't. What the crux of this book is, what I always try to do, is to bridge the gap between professional bartenders and home enthusiasts, and what I have found is that it boils down to . . . you guessed it! Technique. It's the one thing that separates *meh* cocktails from *great* ones.

SHAKING

The good news is that there is no wrong way to shake. As long as you shake a cocktail as hard as you can for eight to ten seconds, you'll achieve everything you need to for a good drink. That said, there is something of an art to it, and it's helpful to know why you're doing it at all. What is the purpose of shaking?

Shaking cocktails is about three things: chilling, dilution, and aeration (texture). Shaking is also the most efficient way to chill and dilute a cocktail: you can achieve equilibrium (optimal dilution and chill) within ten seconds when shaking a cocktail as opposed to stirring, which can take up to two minutes. Shaking properly will also aerate the drink, resulting in a frothy texture a little like a milkshake. In the end, what you want is a drink with twenty-five to thirty percent dilution at around 21°F (-6°C) with a nice frothy head. Simple enough?

HERE'S HOW TO SHAKE

Start by building your cocktail in the tin; if you're using a tin set (which I recommend), I always build the drink in the small tin. Add ice to the larger tin—you'll want a big scoop of ice, somewhere between ¼ to ½ cup (35 to 70 g). Marry the small tin into the big tin, then seal them together by giving them a firm smack with your fist. When shaking, it's helpful to remember not to shake too high, as it puts undue pressure on your rotator cuff. Shaking is a violent action, and you should try to head off any possible injury where you can. Grab the locked tins by the top and bottom and shake, extending your arms from the middle of your chest out in a straight line. Then shake as hard as you can for eight to ten seconds, and you're done. When you're ready to separate the tins, give them a firm tap on the side, right where they meet, to unlock them. Use a Hawthorne strainer to strain the drink.

It bears mentioning that there are a few different styles of shake depending on what kind of drink you're making and what kind of ice you're using.

LONG SHAKE

This is the same shake detailed on page 38. Add ice and shake 8 to 10 seconds before straining into your glass.

WHIP SHAKE

The whip shake is intended for use with pebble or crushed ice cocktails. This shake is done with a little pebble ice (about an ounce) and is intended to add a very targeted amount of dilution to the cocktail, as well as chill it rapidly. This shake also adds a superior amount of aeration to the cocktail, as well as mixing it very thoroughly. Once ice is added, simply shake until the ice has completely melted and you can't hear it in the tin anymore, roughly 20 seconds, then pour the contents into your glass.

SHORT SHAKE

This method is exactly what it says it is, a very short shake. It is usually employed when shaking cocktails with ice of questionable quality and is intended to avoid over dilution but still achieve the right chill.

ROLL

This is less a shake than a mellow way of mixing a drink. It's used for drinks like the Bloody Mary that need to be mixed well but don't need any aeration. To roll a cocktail, you simply pass the cocktail back and forth between tins a few times until the drink is sufficiently mixed.

THROW

You won't find any throwing technique in this book, but it has become a very popular way to make a Martini nowadays, so I'll tell you about it. This technique is incredibly popular with European bartenders. Throwing is just like rolling, but you are pouring the cocktail from one tin to another from a great height. Typically, you raise the glass or tin with the cocktail in it over your head and pour it into another tin held down by your waist. This technique mixes and adds aeration but in a less violent way than shaking. It preserves the top notes of the spirit as well as the silky texture but still adds air, which helps some botanical elements to heighten. This technique is used in lieu of stirring for aromatic cocktails and to add a bit of drama to your presentation. When throwing, be very careful to start the tins close together and pull them apart as you pour from one tin to another. Take it slow! The last thing you want is a cocktail down the front of your shirt!

SHAKING WITH EGGS

You will find several classes of drinks that call for the use of raw egg, such as sours, fizzes, and flips. Shaking with egg calls for a bit of a different shake because these drinks require the maker to play up the texture and limit dilution as much as possible—especially on drinks that only use the white where too much water will kill the foam you've worked so hard to create. The best way of doing this is to shake the cocktail with rock ice. The size of the ice will limit dilution and give it superior foam. There are those who think this technique limits dilution too much, so it can be helpful to add in one piece of cube ice to add in a little more water.

When shaking with rock ice, make sure the rock is fully tempered (allow it to sweat); ice just out of the freezer is brittle, and if you shake with it, it'll shatter in the tin defeating the point altogether. The first step is to shake the tin dry (without ice) for at least 30 seconds—this will whip the eggs into a merengue. Next, add in your tempered rock ice and shake again until you can't hear the cheater cube in the tin (around 15 seconds), then strain into the glass.

Some people like to do what's called a *Reverse Dry Shake* which is literally doing the same steps as above in the opposite order. So, first you shake with ice (you can used cubed ice, no need for rock), then you strain into the small part of the tin, discard the ice, and dry shake last. Many people swear this will give superior foam and it's a bit easier for the beginner.

It also bears mentioning that there are some risks involved when using raw eggs in drinks. Many people think that because the drink contains alcohol, the alcohol will kill bacteria, which, although true, alcohol doesn't kill bacteria on contact—it takes weeks to achieve this. You can always use pasteurized eggs in place of fresh ones, and it'll work fine. For those of you who're feeling more adventurous, use the freshest eggs possible. A good test of egg freshness is to submerge it in a cup of water: Fresh eggs will sink, semi-fresh eggs (but still usable) will sink but stand on their end, and completely unusable eggs will float. Although it may seem nuts to use fresh eggs, I've been working for well over a decade behind bars, and I've never seen anyone get sick. But as with all fun things in life, there are risks associated. Consider yourself informed.

STIRRING

If shaking is the most efficient way of diluting and chilling, then stirring is the least. So why do we do it? What's the point? There are two main reasons. The first is texture. Where shaking causes aeration in the tin, stirring is for drinks that don't need that agitation. Another reason for stirring is to preserve the delicate flavors in spirits like gin, liqueurs, vermouths, and other fortified wines. Many of these spirits have a delicate balance of botanicals in their flavor profile, and when you shake, you dissipate the top notes of flavor, losing these nuances.

For stirring, over-dilution of the drink isn't as much a concern as it is with shaking. Because it's such an inefficient way of chilling and diluting, it would take up to two full minutes to achieve the same equilibrium as a shaken cocktail. No cocktail, with very few exceptions, is stirred for over 45 seconds, so they aren't as cold or diluted as a shaken drink. This is fine with drinks like an Old Fashioned, which sits on ice, because it'll get a little colder and more diluted over time. But for drinks like the Manhattan or Martini, which are served up, there's a little more artistry to getting the drink where it should be.

How to Stir

First, build your cocktail in the glass you intend to stir in; if you don't have a proper stirring glass, a pint glass works well. Next, I like to take the first cube of ice and crack it before putting it in the mixing glass. This will create non-uniform pieces of ice (and some shards) that melt a little quicker, helping with dilution. Then add in a good amount of ice, filling the stirring glass maybe three-quarters full. Next, slide the barspoon down the side of the glass so it rests in between the ice and the glass. Hold the spoon between your pointer finger and ring finger, locking it in place with your thumb. Stir slowly by moving your wrist in a tight circle, causing the spoon to rotate the ice. Make sure to hold the glass in place with your free hand so it doesn't spill, and make sure the back of the spoon is always on the back of the glass. Stir at a slow and steady pace for 30 to 45 seconds, or until you see the outside of the mixing glass frost. Place a julep or Hawthorne strainer into the glass, cupping the ice to strain the drink. See? That wasn't so hard, was it? If your stirring isn't completely smooth at first, that's okay! Just keep practicing, I promise you'll be a pro in no time!

CHAPTER 3

The Sling

When looking at the evolution of cocktails, many people love to point to a specific creation story—something to tie it up neatly with a bow that helps us understand what it is that we're drinking and helps us feel more connected to it. And yet, throughout most of their history, cocktails were deemed not so important when it came to written documentation. Thus, it follows that the information we have on many of the classics is spotty at best, and filled with fanciful stories and conjecture.

Most bartenders who reference the very beginnings of cocktails begin with the Old Fashioned. And that is sensible for a lot of reasons. First, it's a very important cocktail; second, it is incredibly popular (maybe a little less so than in the early days of the modern cocktail rediscovery, but it is a household name). And third, when you trace its history, you find that the build of the cocktail is based on the very definition of how the word *cocktail* was defined at its inception.

BUT, and I had to put this in caps because it is a very big BUT, the Old Fashioned isn't the very beginning of cocktails as we know them. To discover this, you have to start with Punch and then the Sling. This book, however, is organized around cocktails and not large format drinks, so we're going to ignore Punch for the moment and start with the Sling—a drink not many people really pay attention to, and one that has been relegated to a footnote in cocktail history. I mean, you could argue it isn't even a cocktail; it's a slapdash drink that predates cocktails by a good number of years. You could say it doesn't hold much modern relevance; you won't find it on any modern menus save for the obscure, so why pay attention to it?

Note All of the recipes in this book yield one drink.

It stands to reason that many people attempting to write about cocktails pass over this drink because there really isn't that much known about it. Online searches don't reveal too much as far as its history goes. Some people believe the drink popped up in the late 1800s as a prototype to the Highball, which couldn't possibly be true, as we have direct evidence that a bittered Sling existed at least as early as 1806, where it is mentioned in an Upstate New York newspaper called *The Balance Columbian & Repository*. In an article dated May 3, the paper defined cocktails as: *"A stimulating liquor composed of spirits of any kind, sugar, water, and bitters. It is vulgarly called a bittered sling and is supposed to be an excellent electioneering potion because it renders the heart stout and bold, at the same time that it fuddles the head."*

The term "bittered sling" presupposes that a Sling existed before someone decided to bitter it. It's likely that the Sling was around at the very beginning of American distillation, or even before, and was created to choke down rotgut spirits. Back before distilling was the art we know of today, the spirits produced in the late eighteenth century through the mid-nineteenth century were rough and mean and barely drinkable. So, the Sling was developed to make it easy to drink. Add a little water to proof it down and take away the burn, then a little sugar to sweeten it, and presto chango you have a nice-tasting little drink to usher you into oblivion.

If you're anything like me, you want understanding. And to get understanding, you need a sense of where things started. The Old Fashioned was not a cocktail that just popped up out of the ether, it was more of an evolution. This idea is supported not only by its very name but also by the most popular story of its creation. Even though that story was debunked by the brilliant cocktail historian David Wondrich, if you look closely at the drinks that came before it, you can see that this one idea holds true. When tracing the origin of early cocktails, you'll begin to see that the Sling has its fingerprints on a good number of them, not just the Old Fashioned. Since its creation, the Sling split into a few different drink categories. The Sling is Patient Zero. Without it, cocktails would be a completely different thing.

Slings can be made with any spirit. Their construction is much less regimented than the cocktails of today, which in truth can lead to a lot of confusion. Modern drinkers really like to put cocktails into strict, immovable structures as a way of understanding them better. But the early drinks were more of a means to an end rather than a list of finite ingredients. This is a good thing; this is how things evolve, and it's also how we got from a very simple slapdash drink to the multitude of cocktails we have today. We would do well to take a page from this approach.

Historically, the Sling was a drink served in a taller glass with water providing a lot of length to the drink. The Bittered Sling was then a departure from this, and the first step in the evolution of the Whiskey Cocktail and Old Fashioned. According to Wondrich, during the 1800s, the only difference between the Sling and the Toddy was that the Sling was served with a bit of nutmeg grated over the top. Either drink could be served hot or cold, and both had a good amount of water added. For the purpose of my recipe, I have shortened the Sling to resemble its Old Fashioned counterpart. It makes more sense to lengthen it much less since we aren't working our way around unpalatable spirits like they were in the nineteenth century.

Sling Base

Ingredients

1 teaspoon	**Caster sugar**
1 ounce (30 ml)	**Water**
2 ounces (60 ml)	**Old Tom gin**
Garnish	**Whole nutmeg**

Bittered Sling

Ingredients

1 teaspoon	**Caster sugar**
1 ounce (30 ml)	**Water**
2 ounces (60 ml)	**Old Tom gin**
2 or 3 dashes	**Angostura bitters**
Garnish	**Whole nutmeg**

Preparation

To a double old fashioned glass, add the sugar and water and stir to dissolve the sugar.

Next, add the Old Tom gin, and if making a Bittered Sling, the bitters.

Add a large rock of ice and stir for approximately 45 seconds. You could stir this in a mixing glass and strain over ice, but I find this much quicker and just as elegant.

Grate a bit of nutmeg over the top.

The Mid-Century Old Fashioned

This Old Fashioned emerged sometime in the 1950s and became the go-to Old Fashioned during the post-Prohibition time commonly referred to as the Dark Ages of Cocktails. Prohibition destroyed cocktail culture in America, and many of the talented people plying their trade behind the stick either moved away to Europe or quit. When Prohibition lifted, many of the old techniques were lost, and bar owners turned to modern, unhealthy products and eschewed house-made products made with fresh ingredients to save time and money. Although many professionals in polite cocktail society look down on this cocktail build, it does have its charms. This spec is from the godfather of cocktails himself, Dale DeGroff. It was the most prevalent Old Fashioned build from the 1980s up until the modern cocktail revival, and in my opinion it's worth knowing. Although this cocktail is usually made with crappy neon maraschino cherries and ice that will overdilute, this is a craft option and makes a fantastic drink.

Ingredients

¼ ounce (7.5 ml)	**Simple Syrup** (page 28)
2 or 3 dashes	**Angostura bitters**
2	**Orange wheel halves** (one for garnish)
2	**Luxardo cherries** (one for garnish)
2 ounces (60 ml)	**Whiskey**

Preparation

To an old fashioned glass, add the simple syrup, bitters, one orange wheel half, and one Luxardo cherry and muddle. You want to make sure you muddle the flesh of the orange and avoid the peel so as not to extract bitter flavors from the pith.

Add the whiskey and ice (you'll want cubed ice or Kold-Draft for this drink). Stir until sufficiently chilled, approximately 45 seconds.

Garnish with the remaining orange wheel half and cherry.

Sazerac

The Sazerac is a cocktail that has a lot of debate surrounding it. Nobody can agree on the original build or the history of when it came about. It's a long and convoluted tale surrounding a Creole pharmacist named Antoine Amedee Peychaud, an importer of a Cognac called Sazerac de Forge et Fils named Sewell Taylor, and a coffee house called The Sazerac House. What we know for sure is that it emerged sometime between 1850 and 1859 in New Orleans and that although the modern recipe calls for rye whiskey, it's very likely it was first created with Cognac.

My preferred recipe is a split base of Cognac and rye. Together these spirits make this cocktail sing. Making it with one or the other leaves the cocktail a bit flat in my opinion. I tend to also build my Sazeracs with a sugar cube. I feel that this cocktail, too, benefits from the evolution of slowly dissolving sugar. It is not a cocktail that sits on ice, however, and the grainy quality is not to everyone's liking, so I'll forgive you if you would like to use simple syrup (just this one time). The choice of sugar is also important here, as sugars with different levels of refinement will add new flavors. I tend to use white sugar because I love its sharp quality on the palate, but demerara is a good choice to bring in a little molasses flavor and bring out the barrel notes in the spirits. I also tend to put my absinthe in an atomizer because it makes it easier to get an even coat of absinthe on the inside of the glass.

Ingredients

1	**Sugar cube**
4 dashes	**Peychaud's bitters**
Dash	**Club soda**
1 ounce (30 ml)	**Rye whiskey**
1 ounce (30 ml)	**Cognac**
Rinse	**Absinthe**
Garnish	**Lemon twist**

Preparation

To a mixing glass, add the sugar cube and douse with the bitters and a small dash of club soda. Muddle until it forms a paste. You want to make sure to crush the sugar nicely but not completely.

Then add the spirits and some ice and stir until chilled, approximately 45 seconds. Next, grab a neat or footed rocks glass and spray evenly with the absinthe.

Add the rye and Cognac to the glass.

Finally, zest the lemon over the drink and place on top of the glass to garnish.

Fancy Free

The first known reference to the Fancy Free comes from *Crosby Gage's Cocktail Guide and Ladies Companion*, first published in 1940. It essentially takes a page from the Improved Whiskey Cocktail (see page 49) of the late 1800s that swapped liqueur for sugar syrup. The addition of maraschino liqueur gives the drink a dry sweetness, while the orange bitters and orange twist give it a citrus kick.

Ingredients

2 dashes	**Angostura bitters**
1 dash	**Orange bitters**
½ ounce (15 ml)	**Maraschino liqueur**
2 ounces (60 ml)	**Whiskey**
Garnish	**Orange twist**

Preparation

To a cocktail mixing glass, add the bitters, maraschino liqueur, and whiskey along with some ice and stir until sufficiently chilled, about 45 seconds.

Strain into a chilled coupe or cocktail glass and zest the orange twist over the drink.

Garnish with the orange peel.

To Mix or to Mix and Pour?

There are two main ideas about the best way to make an Old Fashioned. Both are correct and will leave you with a fine drink. It's all about how you want your drink to evolve and the presentation of how your drink is perceived. Do you build your Old Fashioned in the glass you're going to drink it from? Or build it in a mixing glass, stir, then strain over a rock of ice? I always tell the bartender to take into consideration the type of bar they're working in. Do you need to get drinks out quickly? Or is it slower where customers are paying more attention to what you're doing? I tend to teach building straight in the glass for bartenders who work in busy environments and need to get drinks out quickly. For those who work in fine dining and higher-end bars, or even for entertaining at home, building in a mixing glass and straining over a beautiful piece of ice is the way to go. There's less stress in that environment, and it's more important to make each drink a bit of a show.

Cock N' Bull Special

This is an Old Fashioned variation that I used to love pulling out in the bar for those patrons who were convinced they've had 'em all. It is such a satisfying drink. I have made so many Cock N' Bull fans over the years, even stubborn patrons who think they know what they want and won't deviate from their pattern. This is the namesake cocktail of a once-popular Hollywood bar, the Cock N' Bull Tavern. The Cock N' Bull is most famous as the birthplace of the ever-popular Moscow Mule. The bar, like many in Hollywood, had celebrity fans such as author Sommerset Maugham and Rod Stewart. It was opened by proprietor Jack Morgan in 1937 and finally shut its doors in 1987 at exactly fifty years old.

Ingredients

2 dashes	**Angostura bitters**
¾ ounce (22 ml)	**Benedictine**
½ ounce (15 ml)	**Cognac**
¼ ounce (7.5 ml)	**Curacao**
¾ ounce (22 ml)	**Rye whiskey**
Garnish	**Orange zest**

Preparation

To your favorite old fashioned glass, add the bitters, Benedictine, Cognac, curacao, and whiskey along with a big rock of ice.

Stir until sufficiently chilled and diluted, about 45 seconds, then zest the orange peel over the cocktail and place it into the drink.

If you under stir this drink, that's okay, it's sitting on a rock of ice that will dilute it as it sits.

Old Devil

Rum Old Fashioneds are ubiquitous in bars these days. That just wasn't so when Danny Cymbal of Cole's French Dip in Downtown Los Angeles came up with this banger. The real strength here is the technique of blending rums for desired effect. I typically don't call out brands in recipes, but rums are so unique in flavor profile that I'm going to have to do it here. If you don't have access to these specific rums, then match the rum style and play around. That's part of the fun anyway, isn't it?

Ingredients

1	**Demerara sugar cube**
4 dashes	**Angostura bitters**
8 drops	**Bittermen's Elemakule Tiki bitters**
1 dash	**Club soda**
1 ounce (30 ml)	**Appleton Estate 12 year Jamaican rum**
¾ ounce (22 ml)	**Sailor Jerry Spiced rum**
¾ ounce (22 ml)	**Smith & Cross Overproof Jamaican rum**
Garnish	**Orange twist**

Preparation

To an old fashioned glass, add the sugar cube and douse with the bitters.

Next, add a tiny dash of club soda and muddle the sugar until it forms a slightly grainy paste.

Add in the rums along with a rock of ice and stir until chilled, about 45 seconds.

Zest the orange peel over the cocktail and garnish the glass with it.

Note

While stirring, it helps to lift the ice gently in the glass to get a good idea of how much sugar has dissolved into the drink. You want to stir so that most of the sugar is gone, but a little remains so the drink gets sweeter as it dilutes.

Oaxaca Old Fashioned

Death & Co is one of the most influential bars to come out of what some people refer to as the "Drinks Renaissance" that took hold in New York in the late 2000s and spread globally. And although there isn't one thing you could credit their success to, the philosophy of sourcing the best products to make exquisite cocktails and developing some of the best talent in the industry was a big part of it. Death & Co gave birth to not only some of the most iconic modern classic cocktails but also some of the most influential people in the industry.

The Oaxaca Old Fashioned was my entry point to Death & Co cocktails. It is the very first one I remember having, and it was, in its day, the only Old Fashioned riff using agave spirits. Mezcal was then largely unknown in the United States and tequila had yet to enjoy the popularity it does today. It was drinks like this that helped to push the popularity of agave spirits.

Ingredients

2 dashes	**Angostura bitters**
1 teaspoon	**Agave nectar**
1½ ounces (45 ml)	**Reposado tequila**
½ ounce	**Mezcal** (see Note)
Garnish	**Orange twist**

Preparation

To an old fashioned glass, add the bitters, agave, tequila, and mezcal along with a big rock of ice and stir until combined and the cocktail is chilled, about 45 seconds.

Zest the orange peel over the cocktail and place it into the drink.

Note

Be very careful what type of mezcal you use in this drink. Like rum, mezcal is very singular in flavor profile, as it is made with several different types of agave plant. The original version of this drink uses Del Maguey San Luis Del Rio mezcal. This is a rather expensive expression at about seventy-five bucks a bottle, so I usually substitute it with Del Maguey Vida and that works well. Whatever mezcal you use, just make sure to use espadin, the most used varietal of mezcal and the most prevalent in cocktails—do that and you're in the right ballpark.

Strawberry Fields Old Fashioned

Strawberry Fields is an original take on an Old Fashioned with the intention of making a delicious, summery Old Fashioned featuring gin. At the time, I had a large crop of lemon balm growing in my garden that gave off the most wonderful aroma. My bar manager at the time, Brent Falco, suggested that I pair it with strawberry while I was trying to figure out a way to get it in the cocktail. What resulted was one of the most delicious syrups I've ever made. This cocktail gives off spring vibes without giving up the heavy sweetness of an Old Fashioned. The lemon balm pairs brilliantly with the botanicals present in gin.

Although any gin will suffice in this recipe, I highly recommend Plymouth if you can find it. Although Plymouth is a lot like London Dry, it has an earthiness in its flavor profile that works wonders in this cocktail.

Ingredients

4 dashes	**Angostura bitters**
½ ounce (15 ml)	**Strawberry Lemon Balm Syrup** (page 33)
2 ounces (60 ml)	**Plymouth gin**
1	**Lemon for zesting**
Garnish	**Thinly sliced strawberries**

Preparation

To an old fashioned glass, add the bitters, syrup, and gin along with a big rock of ice and stir until chilled, diluted, and the syrup combines with the spirits and bitters, about 45 seconds.

With a peeler, pull a strip of lemon and zest over the cocktail then discard.

Garnish with a few thinly sliced strawberries.

American Trilogy

The American Trilogy is probably one of the most famous modern classic cocktails in the Old Fashioned style. It is everything that I look for in a riff: It breaks the template down nicely and shows you just how much can be achieved when sticking to the original ratios and not giving into the temptation to do something crazy. This drink employs a split base, expertly playing the main spirits off each other to give the drinker a complex, yet nuanced experience. It reveals itself layer by layer as the drink slowly dilutes, evolving in the glass. If you're into creating riffs on drinks, the American Trilogy is the gold standard.

I like to think of this drink as the story of early America in a glass. It uses a split base of rye whiskey, America's first whiskey, and apple brandy (also known as applejack), America's first spirit, and, of course, demerara sugar, an incredibly important commodity in early America to complete the trilogy.

I prefer to use Rittenhouse Bonded rye and Laird's Bonded applejack when making this drink. Rittenhouse is a corn-heavy rye that is going to play up a lot of sweet bourbon notes and will forgo a lot of the picklish and bready notes many don't like in rye whiskey. As for the applejack, matching the 100 proof is going to help those more delicate flavors stand up to the rye. Laird's is the original company making applejack in America, founded in 1780 in Scobeyville, New Jersey, it is a relic of colonial times, still family operated and still in production. If you have trouble finding applejack, or it's not sold in your area, you can substitute with calvados. Just make sure you're getting the good stuff: VSOP or above.

The American Trilogy was created by New York City bartenders Michael McIlroy and Richard Boccato while they were at Milk & Honey in 2006.

Ingredients

1	**Demerara sugar cube**
2 dashes	**Orange bitters**
Dash	**Club soda**
1 ounce (30 ml)	**Rye whiskey**
1 ounce (30 ml)	**Applejack**
Garnish	**Orange zest**

Preparation

To an old fashioned glass, add the sugar cube and douse with the bitters and a tiny dash of club soda. With the back of a bar spoon or a muddler, muddle the sugar into a slightly gritty paste.

Then add in the rye and applejack along with a big rock of ice and stir until chilled, about 45 seconds. Zest the orange peel over the glass and garnish with it.

Expanding the Template

Some people call them extended family and others call them kissing cousins. Whatever your name for them, there are a whole class of drinks that popped up around the same time as (or a little before) the Sling that deserve your attention. They're embodied in the Toddy, Julep, Smash, and Cobbler. Confusingly, many of the first cocktails were almost identical to one another, separated only by a single ingredient or even something as negligible as the temperature of the drink. Other times, the drinks *are* the same drink but are known as different things in different regions. Although we are better at categorizing drinks today, we still suffer from this a little bit, and this fact causes a lot of confusion around cocktails. In my mind, Slings branched into two separate categories: The first was the Sling with the addition of bitters, which eventually became the Old Fashioned. The rest are descendants of the Sling as taller, more diluted drinks, and that's where these come in. In truth, some of these in the modern day can be filed under Sours or Highballs, but some, like the Mint Julep, are closer to the Old Fashioned and hard to categorize neatly. Anyway, I'd like to not rob these of their place in history and show them as the extension of that second arm of Slings.

WHISKEY SMASH

According to cocktail historian David Wondrich, the Smash emerged sometime in the 1840s, and by the 1850s, it was one of the most popular drinks. The Smash is essentially a Mint Julep with the addition of muddled fruit. Modern bartenders like to muddle the fruit and double strain the bits out; I personally like to muddle it all together and dump the contents—fruit and all—into the glass and top it off with ice. It's a bit more barbaric, but honestly, I think that's what the spirit of this early drink is.

One technique I have employed that I think makes this drink is muddling a sugar cube with the fruit and cutting back on the simple syrup. The small amount of syrup will immediately work to balance the lemon, but the muddled sugar cube won't dissolve right away, making a cocktail that will evolve from a little on the tart side to a little on the sweet side as you drink. This evolution, when done well, is what makes cocktails so pleasurable to drink.

Dillinger Smash

The Dillinger Smash is a drink I came up with while developing flavors for a company that made bottled cocktails. Always on the lookout for new and exciting flavor pairings, especially those that seem like they don't fit together but do, I found the combination of dill and peach. Not flavors you'd expect to be buddies, but when you taste the combo—oooh mama!

Ingredients

3 to 4	**Sprigs fresh dill** (save one for garnish)
4	**Lemon wedges**
¾ ounce (22 ml)	**Orgeat** (see page 31)
½ ounce (15 ml)	**Peach liqueur**
1½ ounces (45 ml)	**Gin**

Preparation

To a cocktail shaker, add the dill and lemon wedges; make sure the lemon is added peel side down.

Muddle the lemon, crushing it, but being careful to only press the peel and dill to release oils and aroma.

Next, add the orgeat, peach liqueur, and gin along with ice and shake 8 to 10 seconds.

Strain into an old fashioned glass over cubed Ice.

Garnish with a dill sprig.

Whiskey Smash

The Smash is essentially a Julep prepared by muddling mint and shaking it with ice as opposed to stirring it—that was the distinction. Although it first appeared in print in Jerry Thomas's *How to Mix Drinks or The Bon Vivant's Companion* in 1862, cocktail historian David Wondrich says it emerged sometime in the 1840s. Since its inception, the Smash has evolved with the addition of citrus, which is the drink we know today. It is essentially a Mint Julep with the addition of citrus, usually lemon in the form of wedges. Some recipes strain these out, some don't. I prefer my Smashes with all the fruit and shredded mint in the glass.

Ingredients

8 to 10	**Mint leaves**
4	**Lemon wedges**
½ ounce (15 ml)	**Simple Syrup** (page 28)
1	**Sugar cube**
2 ounces (60 ml)	**Whiskey**
1 ounce (28 g)	**Pebble or crushed ice**
Garnish	**Mint bouquet** (see page 35)

Preparation

To a cocktail shaker, add the mint and lemon wedges, peel side down, along with the simple syrup and sugar cube. Having the lemons on top of the mint will allow you to crush the lemon to extract the juice while gently pressing the mint to release its oils. Make sure to crush the sugar cube as well.

Add the whiskey and ice and whip shake (see page 39) until you don't hear any ice in the tin. Dump contents into a larger volume rocks glass and top with pebble ice until you have a small snow cap on top. Garnish with a mint bouquet.

45% Alc/Vol

Mint Julep

The history of the Mint Julep is hazy at best. Some say it got its start in the Arab world, and that its name derives from the Arabic drink *Joulab* and was made with water and rose petals. As the drink moved into the Mediterranean, the rose petals were replaced with mint and the proto-Mint Julep was born.

Juleps surfaced in America in the 1770s—almost exclusively as prescriptions for medicinal purposes. Through the early 1800s, the Mint Julep was considered a morning drink to stimulate the constitution and treat aches and pains. These early Juleps were likely made with brandy, rum, or a mixture of the two. It wouldn't start being made with whiskey until it travelled from north to south, partially because of the Whiskey Rebellion, which took place between 1791 and 1794.

Although the Mint Julep became the official drink of the Kentucky Derby in 1939, it was served at the first Derby in 1875. It's also rumored that Meriwether Lewis Clark Jr., the founder of Churchill Downs, grew mint behind the club.

Ingredients

8 to 10	**Mint leaves**
2 ounces (60 ml)	**Bourbon**
¼ ounce (7.5 ml)	**Simple Syrup** (page 28)
1	**Sugar cube**
1 ounce	**Pebble or crushed ice, plus more for topping**
Garnish	**Mint bouquet** (see page 35), **Powdered sugar** (optional)

Preparation

To the bottom of a julep chalice or double old fashioned glass, add the mint, and then the bourbon, simple syrup, and sugar cube. Using the back of a bar spoon or muddler, lightly muddle the mint—don't use too much force, or you'll add the vegetal flavors from the mint, which will ruin the drink. A light press will break up the sugar and release the desired flavors from the mint leaves.

Once the sugar is broken up, add a scoop of pebble or crushed ice just to the top of the glass. Give it a light stir to dissolve a bit of the sugar (but not all of it). Then, top with more pebble or crushed ice to create a snow cap.

Garnish with a big bushy mint bouquet and powdered sugar (if using). The powdered sugar is entirely optional but gives the mint a nice, frosted look. Give the mint bouquet a light crushing with your fingers to release the oils so the drinker gets the full effect of the mint. Don't slap it too hard or, again, you'll release chlorophyll from the leaves and get a weird vegetal flavor that should be avoided at all costs.

Prescription Julep

This recipe was found by David Wondrich and subsequently added to his book *Imbibe*. It was first published in *Harper's Monthly* in 1857, and its name is a tip of the hat to the original function of the Julep, which was served as medicine.

Ingredients

8 to 10 leaves	**Mint**
1½ ounces (15 ml)	**Cognac**
½ ounce (15 ml)	**Rye whiskey**
¼ to ½ ounce (7.5 to 15 ml)	**Simple Syrup** (page 28)
1 ounce (28 g)	**Pebble or crushed ice, plus more for topping**
Garnish	**Mint bouquet** (see page 35)

Preparation

To the bottom of a julep chalice or double old fashioned glass, add the mint and then the Cognac, rye, and simple syrup.

Using the back of a bar spoon or muddler, lightly muddle the mint, careful to only express the oils from the mint without shredding it.

Add in a scoop of pebble or crushed ice just to the top of the glass. Give it a light stir, then top up with more pebble or crushed ice to create a snow cap.

Garnish with a big bushy mint bouquet.

Toddy (Historic)

Confusingly, the Toddy is basically the exact same thing as a Sling. Although most people are acquainted with the perennially popular Hot Toddy, throughout history Toddies have been made cold as well, for the summer months. So, what's the difference between the Toddy and the Sling? Well, possibly just the name and a bit of nutmeg.

By some accounts, the Toddy cropped up around 1610 in India, and it was the British Empire that brought the drink back to Great Britain. It's possible the name Toddy came from the Hindi word *taddy*, which referred to a beverage made from fermented palm sap. By 1750, the drink had travelled to America and was largely consumed for medicinal purposes.

Although we are used to seeing modern Toddies made with honey and lemon juice, the original contained no citrus whatsoever and was sweetened with anything on hand such as sugar, honey, or molasses. Although it is most commonly made with whiskey, it can be made with any spirit you desire, such as brandy, rum, or even gin, although barrel-aged spirits (Cognac, whiskey, and rums) tend to perform better.

Ingredients

¼ ounce (7.5 ml) **or**	**Simple Syrup** (page 28)
1½ ounces	**Granulated sugar** (see Note)
2 ounces (60 ml)	**Spirit of choice**
3 to 4 ounces (90 to 120 ml)	**Water** (hot or cold)
Garnish	**Ground nutmeg or cinnamon**

Preparation

Temper a mug by filling it with hot water and allow it to warm the mug for a few minutes. (If making a cold toddy, you can skip this step). Dump the water and build your drink. Add the simple syrup or sugar into the mug along with the spirit and give it a slight stir. Add the water to the glass and sprinkle a bit of nutmeg or cinnamon on top. Alternatively, you can add a cinnamon stick to the glass.

Note — If you're using granulated sugar, make sure to dissolve the sugar in a bit of water before adding the other ingredients.

Hot Toddy (Modern)

The modern Toddy is quite different than the historic: These days, we add a bit of citrus to brighten things up and most typically use honey as the sweetener. If you ask for a Hot Toddy at a bar, you're more than likely getting this version.

Ingredients

¾ ounce (22 ml)	**Fresh lemon juice**
¾ ounce (22 ml)	**Honey Syrup** (page 29)
2 ounces (60 ml)	**Scotch**
4 ounces (120 ml)	**Hot water**
Garnish	**None**

Preparation

Repeat the steps for a Hot Toddy on page 69, but remember to use tempered glassware when making hot drinks. You wouldn't want to crack the glass, would you?

Sherry Cobbler

The Cobbler is one of my absolute favorite summer drinks. What many like to call a Porch Sipper, the Cobbler is one of those drinks nobody knows the exact history of; it's thought to have emerged around 1830. What is known is that it became so popular that it supplanted the once dominant Mint Julep. It was, again, cocktail historian David Wondrich who found the earliest known written reference to the drink in the 1838 diary of Katherine Jane Ellice, a Canadian traveler who wrote about it after having one on holiday.

Another interesting historical tidbit that surrounds this drink is that at the time of the Cobbler's popularity, the drinking straw was a recent invention. Early examples were made with uncooked pasta, and it was the Cobbler that bolstered the straw's popularity, making it a household name.

Ingredients

2	**Orange wheel halves**
½ ounce (15 ml)	**Simple Syrup** (page 28)
½ ounce (15 ml)	**Fino sherry**
3 ounces (90 ml)	**Amontillado sherry**
1 ounce (28 g)	**Pebble or crushed ice, plus more for topping**
Garnish	**Mint bouquet** (see page 35) **and seasonal berries**

Preparation

To a cocktail shaker, add the oranges and simple syrup and muddle, being careful not to muddle the peel of the orange, which would impart some bitterness. Next, add both sherries and the pebble or crushed ice. Whip shake (see page 39) and pour, ungated, into a double old fashioned glass. Top with more ice to form a snow cone. Garnish with the mint bouquet and any seasonal berries you have access to.

CHAPTER 4

The Manhattan

The Manhattan is, without question, the red-headed stepchild of the cocktail world. Although it is almost certain that the Manhattan came first, it still plays second fiddle to the more iconic Martini. Popular culture helped the Martini shine, while the Manhattan languished backstage. This could have happened for many reasons, chief among them that the drink is misunderstood and was made in a host of different ways from the start. Although many people declare that the Manhattan was a rye drink at its inception, it was made with both bourbon and rye. This would mean that the bartender making the drink would need to have good working knowledge of both the whiskeys and vermouths used, or the drink could very easily fall flat. And, of course, James Bond made the Martini sexy and dangerous, solidifying its iconic stature. Whatever the reason, a well-made Manhattan is criminally underrated. Although you'll find many books declaring the Martini the root cocktail to the three-ingredient cocktail containing fortified wine, the Manhattan was first. Period. End of discussion.

There are two plausible stories handed down about the genesis of the Manhattan with very little known about the details. It is most likely that it was not only created in the New York borough of Manhattan but also in the Manhattan Club some time in the 1870s. One story is that it was created by a guy named Ian Marshall for a banquet thrown by Jennie Jerome (mother of Winston Churchill) honoring then presidential candidate Samuel J. Tilden. Another was simply that it was created by a bartender named "Black" who owned a bar on Broadway south of Houston Street. Whatever the true story is (we will likely never know), the Manhattan ushered in a whole new way of making cocktails cutting vermouth in as a way to add complexity, but also, in many cases, lower the ABV (alcohol by volume) of the drink so people at the bar could keep their legs as they walked out at the end of the night.

Desert Island Manhattan

My Desert Island Manhattan has a rye whiskey base. Although this is the less popular whiskey in the United States, it makes the best (and most balanced) Manhattan. I also like to use at least 100 proof whiskey; the heat of the proof is going to really accentuate the spice of the rye. And lastly, I like to use a very flavorful and robust vermouth that will stand up to the higher proof whiskey.

Ingredients

4 dashes	**Angostura bitters**
2 ounces (60 ml)	**Rittenhouse rye**
1 ounce (30 ml)	**Carpano Antica sweet vermouth**
3 ounces (90 ml)	**Amontillado sherry**
Garnish	**Luxardo cherry or lemon twist**

Preparation

To a mixing glass, add the bitters, rye, and vermouth along with plenty of ice and stir for about 45 seconds. Strain into a coupe or cocktail glass and garnish with a Luxardo cherry or lemon twist.

Note

You can customize your Manhattans by taking note of your whiskey's mash bill (see page 77). If your rye has a lot of corn in its makeup, you'll know that it will be a little sweeter, less spicy, and generally hit more like a bourbon. The same goes with using bourbons: more rye will make it a bit spicier, and a wheated bourbon will be much softer and sweeter.

Manhattan Variations

The strength of the Manhattan is that it is simply a combination of American whiskey and fortified wine with a few dashes of bitters. This template offers almost unlimited combinations. That said, to make a good one you must understand the flavor profile of the whiskey you're using and the flavors of the fortified wine. Manhattans are typically made with sweet vermouth, which contains a proprietary blend of herbs and spices. No two vermouths are exactly alike and can differ wildly from region to region—especially in today's world where we have small companies making all manner of vermouth. Although this may sound intimidating, it's a great way to experiment and learn; switch out the whiskey and vermouth used to see what happens to the flavors. And the best part about it? You get to drink all the prototypes.

Part of the art of making good Manhattans is selecting a sweet vermouth that pairs well with the whiskey you select for the drink. You need to keep not only the overall profile of the vermouth in mind but also the mash bill of the whiskey—that is, what grains the whiskey is made from and how strong they are (their ABV). For instance, overproof whiskies (those that are 100 proof or over) will have big enough flavors that can run over the delicate nuances of some vermouths; others may be too sweet to pair with bourbon or too dry to pair with a rye. It's difficult to give hard and fast rules for these pairings, as vermouths are proprietary blends of botanicals and no two are exactly alike. And new products are always coming out, pushing the category forward. The basic rule of thumb I use is this: for high-proof spirits I tend to use a very flavorful sweet vermouth such as Carpano Antica, something I know will not get lost in the boldness of the spirit. Drier sweet vermouths will pair well with sweeter whiskey such as bourbon or high-corn rye, and of course, sweeter vermouths will go better with drier whiskies such as rye or high-rye bourbon. Play around, have fun, and drink Manhattans. I leave you to it.

Perfect Manhattan

Back when I was brand new to the industry, this is the drink many bar managers would ask about to weed out people they were interviewing for a job. Since then, with so much information on the internet, the questions have gotten a bit more technical. I can remember at least one interview I flunked for not knowing what a Perfect Manhattan was.

The Perfect Manhattan may very well be the perfect drink. Splitting the vermouth base gives it a little more variety in botanicals, and it cuts the sometimes cloying nature of the sweet vermouth, making the drink a little lighter and less sweet.

Ingredients

2 dashes	**Angostura bitters**
½ ounce (15 ml)	**Sweet vermouth**
½ ounce (15 ml)	**Dry vermouth**
2 ounces (60 ml)	**Bourbon or rye whiskey**
Garnish	**Luxardo cherry or lemon twist**

Preparation

To a mixing glass, add the bitters, vermouths, and bourbon along with plenty of ice and stir for about 45 seconds.

Strain into a coupe or cocktail glass and garnish with a cherry or lemon twist.

The Brooklyn Variations

Starting in the early 2000s, New York bartenders began making a whole slew of Manhattan/Brooklyn riff cocktails for just about every neighborhood in Brooklyn. The trend started with the Red Hook created by early Milk & Honey bartender Vincenzo Errico, and soon many other heavy hitters of the industry had their own—sparking a whole new category of Manhattan riffs celebrating the various boroughs of New York City. This trend didn't stop with New York either: Once these cocktails became known to the greater bartending community, many bartenders from far and wide got in on it and made variations for their cities as well. What we have now is a bonified category of ever-expanding Manhattan riffs. Some of these recipes went on to becoming bona fide modern classics travelling via bar menus all over the globe, and some remain local favorites. For my money, they all stand as a testament to how far you can push creativity in a simple three-ingredient whiskey drink. Following are a few of my favorites, ones that I think not only support what a Manhattan should be at its core but also add something to the category not previously expressed.

Red Hook

The Red Hook was created by Italian bartender Vincenzo Errico in 2005 at the legendary New York City bar Milk & Honey, which is credited for helping to spark the modern-day cocktail revival. Errico met Milk & Honey founder, Sasha Petraske, while Petraske was in London opening the London arm of Milk & Honey. Petraske convinced Errico to come back to New York, and Errico found himself behind the stick at Petraske's bar. Errico is now back in Italy and is the proprietor of his own bar, L'ArteFatto, on the island of Ischia off the coast of Naples. The cocktail is named for the neighborhood of Red Hook Brooklyn, settled by Dutch Colonists in 1636 and now an artistic community right on the water overlooking the Statue of Liberty.

Ingredients

½ ounce (15 ml)	**Punt e Mes**
½ ounce (15 ml)	**Maraschino liqueur**
2 ounces (60 ml)	**Rye whiskey**
Garnish	**Candied cherry**

Preparation

To a mixing glass, add the Punt e Mes, maraschino liqueur, and rye along with plenty of ice and stir for about 45 seconds.

Strain into a coupe or cocktail glass and garnish with a cherry.

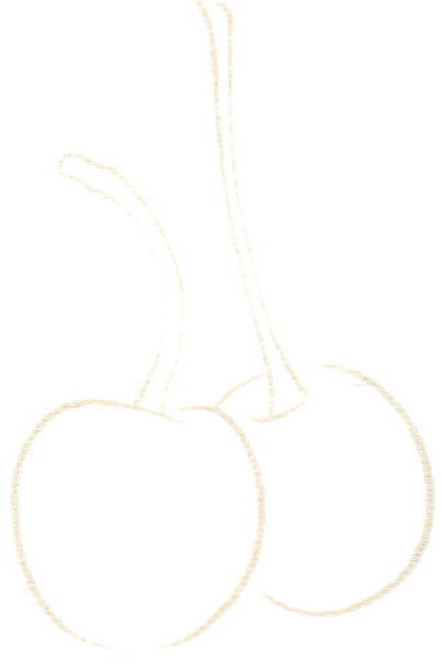

Bensonhurst

The Bensonhurst was created by New York City Bartender Chad Solomon in 2006. At the time, Solomon was bartending at both Milk & Honey as well as the Pegu Club, which was owned by Audrey Saunders and opened the year before.

Ingredients

1 ounce (30 ml)	**Dry vermouth**
2 teaspoons	**Maraschino liqueur**
1 teaspoon	**Cynar**
2 ounces (60 ml)	**Rye whiskey**
Garnish	**None**

Preparation

To a mixing glass, add the vermouth, maraschino liqueur, Cynar, and rye along with plenty of ice and stir for about 45 seconds.

Strain into a coupe or cocktail glass.

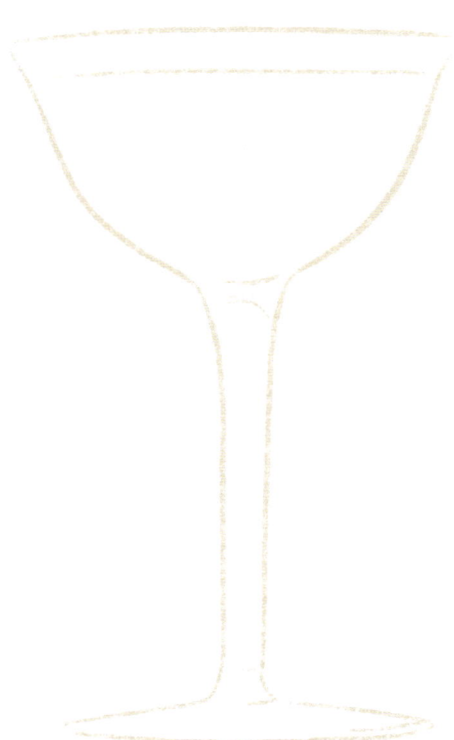

Greenpoint

The Greenpoint was created by bartender Michael McIlroy at Milk & Honey in 2006. McIlroy was one of the early bartenders at Milk & Honey and now co-owns Attaboy, which he founded in 2013 with business partner Sam Ross in the former Milk & Honey space once it closed in 2020.

Ingredients

2 dashes	**Angostura bitters**
1 dash	**Orange bitters**
½ ounce (15 ml)	**Yellow Chartreuse**
2 ounces (60 ml)	**Bourbon or rye whiskey**
½ ounce (15 ml)	**Sweet vermouth**
2 ounces (60 ml)	**Rye whiskey**
Garnish	**Lemon twist**

Preparation

To a mixing glass, add the bitters, Yellow Chartreuse, vermouth, and rye along with plenty of ice and stir for about 45 seconds.

Strain into a coupe or cocktail glass and garnish with a lemon twist.

CHAPTER 5

The Martini

The Martini is without a doubt the most famous of all cocktails. Some may argue that the Old Fashioned comes close in popularity, and while it has always been popular and it did have a big moment right at the beginning of the late 1990s until about 2010—the time many people refer to as the "Modern Cocktail Renaissance"—it has never come near to the Martini. Not even close. For many, the Martini is the epitome of what cocktails represent in our culture: sophistication and sex appeal. That's why of all the drinks that exist, the Martini has permeated pop culture to a degree we've not seen with any other cocktail.

And the Martini is technically a Manhattan riff! That's right! If I had been stubborn enough to deny the Martini its own chapter in this book, it would be tucked right in with the Manhattan. But it's not right to do that; if anything, the Manhattan is the redheaded stepchild to the Martini, always tagging along on menus but never noticed quite as much. Suffice it to say that it has as many, if not more, riffs than the Manhattan, so tucking it away with so many Manhattan riffs would be criminal.

Nobody knows exactly when the Martini was created, and like so many drinks of that era, there are a few competing stories surrounding it. The most credible—and the one cocktail historians accept as the most probable—is that the Martini was likely an evolution of the Martinez. And this stands to reason because the very first printed Martini recipe (that we know of), from Harry Johnson's *New and Improved Bartender's Manual* published in 1888, was a wholly different drink than the dry Martinis we have today. That recipe contained gum syrup, Boker's bitters, and Old Tom gin, which made it dark, much sweeter, and heavy as opposed to the razor-sharp drinks we expect nowadays.

The Martinez

There is no better cocktail to start this chapter with than the Martinez. It is the drink that many point to as the first step in the evolution away from the Manhattan and toward the modern Martini. I have heard a few different stories about how the Martinez came about, but what most historians do agree on is that it evolved from the Manhattan sometime in the mid 1870s. There are two competing stories of its genesis. The first is that legendary bartender Jerry Thomas created the cocktail at the Occidental Hotel for a patron on their way to the city of Martinez, California. The other, and the one touted by the city itself, is that a local bartender by the name of Richelieue created it while working at a saloon in the namesake city. Whatever the truth, it first saw print in O.H. Byron's *The Modern Bartender's Guide,* published in 1884.

If you're thinking about making a more historically accurate version of this cocktail, there is the question as to what type of gin to use in it. According to Difford's Guide, London Dry wasn't widely available in the States during the mid-1870s, but because of the Dutch Colonization of Manhattan in the early 1600s, Dutch Genever was readily available to anyone who wanted to drink it. It's more likely that the first Martinez's were made with something closer to the Dutch style gin. Personally, I like the use of Old Tom, which brings those malty notes and a little added sweetness but still reads as gin.

Ingredients

2 dashes	**Angostura bitters**
¼ ounce (7.5 ml)	**Maraschino liqueur**
1½ ounces (45 ml)	**Sweet vermouth**
1½ ounces (45 ml)	**Old Tom gin**
Garnish	**Orange twist**

Preparation

To a mixing glass, add the bitters, maraschino liqueur, vermouth, and gin along with plenty of ice and stir for about 45 seconds.

Strain into a coupe or cocktail glass and garnish with the orange twist.

Martini (My Preferred Recipe)

This is my standard recipe when I make Martinis for myself, and the one that I push people toward when I advocate for the Martini. In my mind, this one is a bit easier for those that haven't primed their palate for the ultra-boozy drink. The higher volume of dry vermouth knocks the proof down a hair, and the botanical blend between the gin and vermouth is showcased more.

This drink is technically a Martini riff called a Marguerite, but I don't distinguish it that way to those I serve it to. Is it disrespectful to the history of the drink? Maybe. But having a thousand Martini variations is disrespectful to the bartender! As with all Martinis, the choice of vermouth and gin is important. I like to go with Plymouth gin, which is called for in 1904's *Stuarts Fancy Drinks and How to Mix Them*; it has an earthy flavor to it but preserves a lot of the citrus you'll find in a London Dry and Dolin Dry vermouth whose botanicals pair perfectly.

While sipping on this Martini, snack on some Castelvetrano olives and revel in the surprising delight of orange and olives.

Ingredients

1 dash	**Orange bitters**
1 ounce (30 ml)	**Dolin dry vermouth**
2 ounces (60 ml)	**Plymouth gin**
Garnish	**Orange twist**

Preparation

To a mixing glass, add the bitters, vermouth, and gin along with plenty of ice and stir for about 45 seconds.

Strain into a coupe or cocktail glass and garnish with the orange twist.

Note

The orange twist is *my* twist on this drink. If you'd like to make a more accurate Marguerite, use a lemon twist.

Gibson

The Gibson is simply a Martini garnished with a cocktail onion. I always make this drink a little drier—more out of habit than preference—but honestly, it works both ways. It's how I learned the drink, and this is the way I drink them to this day. As far as I know, this drink was created at San Francisco's Bohemian Club in 1898 and was first published in William Boothby's *The World's Drinks and How to Mix Them* in 1908.

Ingredients

¾ ounce (22 ml)	**Dry vermouth**
2¼ ounces (67.5 ml)	**Gin**
Garnish	**Cocktail onion**

Preparation

To a mixing glass, add the vermouth and gin along with plenty of ice and stir for about 45 seconds.

Strain into a coupe or cocktail glass and garnish with the cocktail onion.

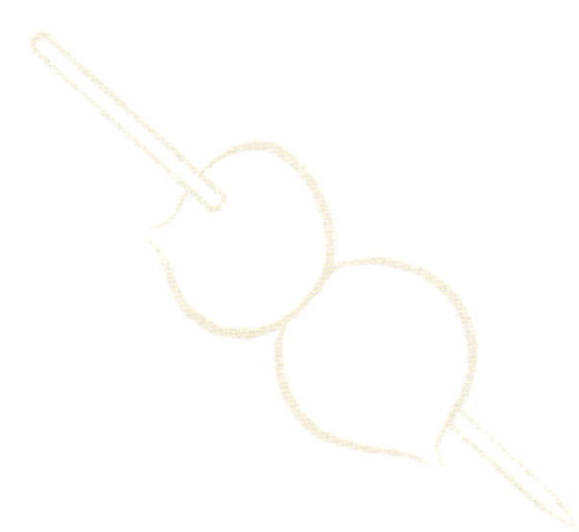

50/50 Martini

This drink, which today is a less popular Martini build, was most probably closer to what people were drinking back in the eighteenth century where the preference was that a Martini should be bone dry and contain little to no vermouth. To me, this ultra-dry Martini does the drinker a massive disservice and is also a product of Americans not understanding that vermouth goes in the fridge. But that's a talk for another day. The fact is that Martinis sing when coupled with good, fresh vermouth, pairing those botanicals with the ones in the gin. Although simple, Martinis can be quite complex. This build was reintroduced to polite society when the Pegu Club in New York City, helmed by early gin advocate Audry Saunders, put it on the menu as the Fitty-Fitty.

Ingredients

2 dashes	**Orange bitters**
1½ ounces (45 ml)	**Dry vermouth**
1½ ounces (45 ml)	**Gin**
Garnish	**Lemon twist**

Preparation

To a mixing glass, add the bitters, vermouth, and gin along with plenty of ice and stir for about 45 seconds.

Strain into a coupe or cocktail glass and garnish with the lemon twist.

Turf Club

Originally published in George Winter's *How to Mix Drinks* in 1884, the Turf Club was one of the first Martini variations. The first publication saw it made with Old Tom gin, making it very similar to a Martinez. But by the time the drink made it into Harry Johnson's *Bartenders Manual*, published in 1900, bartenders had switched the Old Tom for Plymouth gin, which is a bit closer to London Dry in flavor. Personally, I like the crispness of a London Dry with more pronounced juniper for this drink, but if you're a stickler for Plymouth, it will also work well.

Turf Club refers to the Gentleman's club of the same name that stood on the corner of Madison Avenue and 6th Street in Manhattan. The club was a meeting place for the wealthy gentlemen of the day to have a drink, eat fancy food, and gamble away their money.

Ingredients

2 dashes	**Orange bitters**
2 dashes	**Absinthe**
¼ ounce (7.5 ml)	**Maraschino liqueur**
¾ ounce (22 ml)	**Dry vermouth**
2 ounces (60 ml)	**Gin**
Garnish	**Lemon twist**

Preparation

To a mixing glass, add the bitters, absinthe, maraschino liqueur, vermouth, and gin along with plenty of ice and stir for about 45 seconds.

Strain into a coupe or cocktail glass and garnish with the lemon twist.

Kangaroo

The Kangaroo is just a fancy name given to the Vodka Martini by Oscar Haimo in his 1943 book, *Cocktail Digest*. Some (including myself) previously thought that this was the original name given to the Vodka Martini, but it wasn't; it first appeared in print in a Smirnoff ad pamphlet in 1935, a full eight years before Haimo dubbed it the Kangaroo Kicker. That said, I like the name Kangaroo for this cocktail more than the barely serviceable "Vodka Martini," so that's what I always call them.

Ingredients

¾ ounce (22 ml)	**Dry vermouth**
2 ounces (60 ml)	**Vodka**
Garnish	**Lemon twist**

Preparation

To a mixing glass, Add the vermouth and vodka along with plenty of ice and stir for about 45 seconds.

Strain into a Nick & Nora glass and garnish with the lemon twist.

Dirty Vodka Martini

If there is any standard Martini bar order nowadays it is most certainly the Dirty Martini. Although the history of Martinis is muddy with confusion, we have cocktail historian David Wondrich to thank for uncovering the origins of this drink. According to Wondrich, the drink was created by a bartender named John E. O'Connor who came up with this drink while working behind the bar at the Waldorf Astoria hotel in 1901.

Ingredients

¼ ounce (7.5 ml)	**Quality olive brine**
½ ounce (15 ml)	**Dry vermouth**
1¾ ounces (52.5 ml)	**Vodka**
Garnish	**Olive**

Preparation

To a mixing glass, add the olive brine, vermouth, and vodka along with plenty of ice and stir for about 45 seconds.

Strain into a Nick & Nora glass and garnish with an olive or two on a cocktail pick.

CHAPTER 6

The Negroni

The Negroni, in my mind, fits squarely into the Manhattan category. It is a three-ounce (89 ml) drink consisting of a spirit, sweet vermouth, and bitters (in the form of Campari) that is the basic Manhattan template. Not only has it been the genesis of many different riffs, but it also has an evolution that seems to stand apart from the Manhattan. It evolved from a much simpler drink called a Milano Torino, an aperitivo cocktail consisting of sweet vermouth, and Campari. I've never found any evidence to support it as a riff of a Manhattan, so again, it would be criminal not to give it its own chapter.

The Negroni is an almost infinitely riffable template. You have three ingredients: gin, sweet vermouth, and a bitter aperitivo, all of which contain a proprietary blend of herbs, barks, spices, and citrus peels. Switch any one of these ingredients out for another, and you have a very different cocktail each time. And by that token, the elements themselves are so powerful and add so much in juxtaposition to each other that if you even tinker with their volume, your drink will be entirely new. It's an easy drink to have a fresh take on, and almost every bar worth its salt has their own signature Negroni blend.

The Negroni is what I'd call a "professional drink," meaning there are very few people who aren't seasoned drinkers that can approach this drink and actually like it. But like the pediatrician said when my kids were born, "Kids don't know if they like something until they've tried it at least fifteen times," so, too, is most people's experience with the Negroni.

This is a drink that you must put effort into to truly appreciate; it's an acquired taste. It consists of three polarizing ingredients the vast majority of drinkers have convinced themselves they hate. But once you do acquire the taste for it, oh mama! There's nothing better.

This is one of my absolute favorite drinks; it's so rare to encounter something that challenges and expects something from us. My first Negroni was such a visceral experience that I remember the moment like it was yesterday. I went to visit a friend at a new bar he was working at and asked for a Bartender's Choice cocktail, and he handed me my first Negroni. The first sip both repelled and intrigued me. It was like nothing I'd ever tasted. I was instantly obsessed with the drink and trying to understand its flavor profile.

Modern American cocktail culture owes a lot to the Negroni. Nowadays, seeing amaro and other bitter liqueurs in drinks and on menus is common, but that wasn't the case at the time of the Negroni's ascent in modern drinking culture. Americans tended to shrink away from bitter flavors, and it was the crazy popularity of this drink that paved the way for Americans to open their minds to new flavors—it's probably the single reason you see a wealth of amari on the back bar of any self-respecting cocktail bar today. If you hate Negronis, stick with them, prime your palate, and a whole new world will open up to you.

The Negroni is an evolution of two other drinks that don't belong in this section but you will find in this book. The first is the Milano Torino, a simple equal-parts mixture of Campari bitter aperitivo (from Milan) and sweet vermouth (from Turin). This drink is credited to Gaspare Campari, who invented it sometime around 1860 at his own place, Caffe Camparino. Around the same time the Americano also showed up on the scene. There is no historical proof, but this one is credited to Gaspare Campari as well, and the name is a reference to taking the Milano Torino and making it "American Style" by lengthening it with club soda, which was very popular with the American tourists at the time. In turn, the Negroni is credited to a man named Count Camillo Negroni who frequented a café called Café Cassoni in Florence, Italy, around 1919. The story goes that one day Count Camillo asked the bartender to make him an Americano but to replace the club soda with gin to make it a little stronger. The bartender complied and added an orange garnish instead of the customary lemon you get with the Americano, and the Negroni was born.

The Negroni is a pretty forgiving template, and there are many ways to play with the specs to suit it to your liking. Here, I've given you two of the most used ratios: the original and a modern one that cuts the Campari and vermouth in favor of more gin. This drink is almost infinitely customizable: Switching out gins and sweet vermouths for other brands will get you sometimes wildly new flavors due to their proprietary nature. These days, there are many companies that make red aperitivo liqueurs you can sub for the Campari to make slight variations on this drink. Some are sweeter, some are drier, some are more bitter and some are less. Play with it! Although Negronis are indeed an acquired taste for the uninitiated, I do believe there is a Negroni for everyone.

ORIGINAL

Negroni

Ingredients

1 ounce (30 ml)	**Sweet vermouth**
1 ounce (30 ml)	**Campari**
1 ounce (30 ml)	**Gin**
Garnish	**Orange twist**

MODERN

Negroni

Ingredients

¾ ounce (22 ml)	**Sweet vermouth**
¾ ounce (22 ml)	**Campari**
1½ ounces (45 ml)	**Gin**
Garnish	**Orange twist**

Preparation

To a mixing glass, add the vermouth, Campari, and gin along with plenty of ice and stir for around 25 seconds, then strain over a large rock of Ice.

Garnish with the orange twist.

Negroni Sbagliato

The Italian word *sbagliato* roughly translates to "messed up" in English, so the name of this drink is the "Messed-Up Negroni." It was created by bartender Mirko Stocchetto at an establishment called Bar Basso in the 1970s. Bar Basso is famous for being *the* bar to first offer aperitivo drinks to the everyday person. It's a historic bar that opened in 1947 and is still around today. The story goes that during a busy shift, Mirko accidentally grabbed a bottle of Prosecco instead of gin while making a Negroni and sent it out to the guest. The guest loved it, and history was made.

Ingredients

1 ounce (30 ml)	**Campari**
1 ounce (30 ml)	**Sweet vermouth**
1 ounce (30 ml)	**Prosecco**
Garnish	**Orange wheel half**

Preparation

To a rocks glass, add the Campari and vermouth and fill with ice. Add the Prosecco and stir briefly to combine.

Garnish with the orange wheel half.

Boulevardier

One of the best-known riffs of the Negroni, the Boulevardier is credited to an American writer named Erskine Gwynne who moved to Paris and created a literary magazine called *Boulevardier*, which was in circulation from 1927 to 1932. The drink first made its way into print in Harry McElhone's 1927 book *Barflies and Cocktails*. McElhone was the proprietor of Harry's American Bar in Paris, at which Gwynne was a regular.

Ingredients

1 ounce (30 ml)	**Sweet vermouth**
1 ounce (30 ml)	**Campari**
1½ ounces (45 ml)	**Bourbon or rye whiskey**
Garnish	**Orange peel**

Preparation

To a cocktail mixing glass, add the vermouth, Campari, and bourbon along with plenty of ice and stir until sufficiently chilled, about 45 seconds.

Strain into a chilled coupe or cocktail glass, zest the orange over the drink, and place it into the drink.

White Negroni

Invented by bartender Wayne Collins in 2001, the White Negroni is by far the most known and popular Negroni riff. Collins was in Bordeaux, France, at a trade show called VinExpo, and wanted to make Negronis with primarily French ingredients. The swaps made for this drink were very well thought out, and it's easy to see why it became so popular. There are several different builds out there, but I implore you to taste the original, which uses the same structure, just swapping ingredients.

Ingredients

1 ounce (30 ml)	**Lillet blanc**
1 ounce (30 ml)	**Suze**
1 ounce (30 ml)	**Gin**
Garnish	**Lemon twist**

Preparation

To a rocks glass with a big rock of ice, add the Lillet blanc, Suze, and gin and stir until sufficiently chilled, about 45 seconds.

Zest the lemon over the drink and place the peel alongside the ice.

Kingston Negroni

There are very few cocktails that can't be improved with rum, and this Negroni riff is no exception. It was created back in 2009 by New York City bartender and partner at Pouring Ribbons, Joaquin Simó. The drink is as simple as it gets. Simó just plugged rum in the place of gin and created one of the most popular modern riffs on this drink. Sometimes, it's just that easy.

Ingredients

1 ounce (30 ml)	**Overproof aged Jamaican rum** (Pot Still is best)
1 ounce (30 ml)	**Campari**
1 ounce (30 ml)	**Sweet vermouth**
Garnish	**Orange wheel half**

Preparation

To a rocks glass with a big rock of ice, add the rum, Campari, and vermouth and stir until sufficiently chilled, about 45 seconds.

Garnish with the orange wheel half.

Left Hand

Created by bartender Sam Ross around 2006 at Milk & Honey in New York City, the Left Hand is one of a very few good Negroni variations that utilize bourbon as a main spirit. It is the perfect drink to illustrate the connection between Negronis and Manhattans, as this drink is kind of both all in one. Pick chocolate bitters with a little spice, such as Fee's Aztec bitters, to really knock this drink up a notch.

Ingredients

2 dashes	**Chocolate bitters**
¾ ounce (22 ml)	**Sweet vermouth**
¾ ounce (22 ml)	**Campari**
1½ ounces (45 ml)	**Bourbon**
Garnish	**Luxardo cherry**

Preparation

Add all ingredients to a mixing glass with ice and stir until sufficiently chilled, approximately 45 seconds.

Strain into a chilled coupe or cocktail glass and garnish with a Luxardo cherry.

Locals Only

To be honest, I'm a huge fan of this cocktail but not of what I named it after. The name is a reference to a graffiti slogan that originated at the highly coveted surf spots that dot the California coast, warning weekend warriors and out-of-towners they're not welcome. In the context of the drink, it's solely a reference to my use of local California products. The idea with this one was to make a Negroni that amplifies similar flavors of my favorite Martini build and reads like a Martini at the table. A mashup of two of my favorite cocktails.

Ingredients

2 or 3 drops	**Bittermen's Tiki bitters**
¾ ounce (22 ml)	**Vya dry vermouth**
¾ ounce (22 ml)	**Angeleno amaro**
2 ounces (60 ml)	**Mulholland gin**
Garnish	**Orange twist**

Preparation

To a mixing glass, add the bitters, vermouth, amaro, and gin and fill with ice. Stir until sufficiently chilled, about 45 seconds, and strain into a chilled coupe or cocktail glass.

Zest the orange twist over the drink and place it into the glass.

Note

This drink really sings with a cucumber forward gin. I know, though, that many of you won't have access to Mulholland which is not yet in global markets, so you can supplant with Hendrix or Martin Miller gin in those cases.

CHAPTER 7

The Sour

The Sour is without a doubt the most popular cocktail category in the world. And, as such, the largest chapter in this book. Although some stirred cocktails such as Old Fashioneds and Martinis have enjoyed a good amount of popularity, they are outstripped by any Sour on any menu, hands down, end of discussion. Sours are easily palatable for those who may not have acquired the taste for spirits, so it follows that a much larger demographic of people love them.

People have been mixing spirits with citrus and sugar for far longer than the Sour was defined as an official cocktail category. Although the term "Sour" was coined somewhere around 1850, Sours themselves are a stripped-down version of a punch, an alcoholic art that has been around since the early 1600s. Punches were incredibly fashionable in early America, and men would sit drinking punch for hours in punch houses and bars. Then, as the Victorian era began, the pace of life increased and people drank punch less. It wasn't that they didn't want to drink; they just couldn't sit around a Punch House all day getting knackered, and so bartenders began making smaller one-off punches. That way, people could come in on their lunch break, knock off a drink, go back to work, and productivity wouldn't suffer. These drinks were coined by David Wondrich as "Lesser Punches" and very well could be the inception of the sour.

Another true story that is given credit for the creation of the modern Sour surrounds the British Royal Navy. Since 1655, the British

Royal Navy had been giving their soldiers rum rations, a practice that was discontinued in 1970. But back then, rum was given to men in place of a daily beer ration, given that beer tended to go bad and rum did not. By 1739 this had become standard practice, and one gill (equivalent to a quarter of a pint) of rum was given to all sailors. This solved the problem of beer rations going bad but created the new problem of drunkenness. Then, in 1740, an admiral named Edward Vernon proclaimed that all rum rations would be diluted with water and be given twice a day. Around this same time, sailors also realized that limes helped to combat scurvy. So, it became common practice for sailors to mix a little lime and sugar into their rum ration—the lime for scurvy and the sugar to make it more palatable. And there you have a prototype for the modern Sour. These days, the template for the Sour is based on Jerry Thomas's 1862 recipe, which calls for any spirit, any citrus, any sugar, and water. That is the template we go by to this day.

Sours are a little tricky, and their very simple template is a little deceptive. There is a reason that Sours, especially those made with lime, are assigned to prospective bartenders by bar managers as a litmus test for skill behind the bar. The sweetness and tartness of citrus fruit—particularly lemon and lime, the two fruits used in most Sour builds—are variable throughout the year, and the trick to a fantastic Sour is knowing how tart or sweet the citrus you're using is and dialing in the recipe to make up for the missing component. There are two builds for a Sour that take this into consideration and can be used interchangeably to make sure the Sour you build is on point.

To kick off this chapter, I've given you the two main builds for a Sour. One tends to be a little sweeter and the other a little tarter. No matter where you live, even if you're in California and can get most citrus year-round, citrus fluctuates in acidity and sweetness at different times of year. In the spring, when citrus is sweeter, you'll want to use more citrus and less sugar to find the proper balance, and vice versa. I love making this standard spec with gin, as it not only makes for a delicious drink, but also one to reinitiate those who have sworn off gin, but because it's unforgiving and will show flaws in the balance of the cocktail immediately. It's a great one to make in different ways and taste through to learn more about your palate and sense of flavor balance.

TRADITIONAL SWEET

Sour

Ingredients

¾ ounce (22 ml)	**Fresh lemon juice**
¾ ounce (22 ml)	**Simple Syrup** (page 28)
2 ounces (60 ml)	**Any spirit**
Garnish	**Lemon twist**

TRADITIONAL TART

Sour

Ingredients

1 ounce (30 ml)	**Fresh lemon juice**
¾ ounce (22 ml)	**Simple Syrup** (page 28)
2 ounces (60 ml)	**Any spirit**
Garnish	**Lemon twist**

Preparation

To a cocktail shaker, add the lemon juice, simple syrup, and spirit along with ice and shake 8 to 10 seconds.

Double strain into a coupe or cocktail glass and garnish with the lemon twist.

Fix

The Fix is an early drink that can be made with just about any spirit but was historically made with Cognac (or other brandy), Holland's gin, or rum. Back in its day, it was considered a separate class of drink, more of a fancy one-off punch than a sour. It's also quite close to a Cobbler, the only difference being that Cobblers have fruit inside the drink, whereas the Fix solely uses fruit as garnish. Below is a very basic Fix recipe, although using pineapple syrup also works very well.

Ingredients

¾ ounce (22 ml)	**Fresh lemon juice**
¾ ounce (22 ml)	**Simple Syrup** (page 28)
2 ounces (60 ml)	**Old Tom gin**
Garnish	**Mint sprig, seasonal fruits, or lemon peel**

Preparation

To a cocktail shaker, add the lemon juice, simple syrup, and gin along with some crushed ice and whip shake (see page 39).

Dump into a double old fashioned glass and top with more crushed ice. Garnish with mint, fruit, or lemon peel.

Whiskey Sour

Although Sours were made with (and can be made with) a variety of different spirits, the most popular version is without question the Whiskey Sour. Some bartenders will have you believe that the first Whiskey Sours were made with egg white, and while the vast majority of modern Whiskey Sours are, historically speaking, the first ones were not.

Ingredients

¾ ounce (22 ml)	**Fresh lemon juice**
¾ ounce (22 ml)	**Simple Syrup** (page 28)
2 ounces (60 ml)	**Whiskey**
2 or 3 dashes	**Angostura bitters**
Garnish	**Lemon wheel half and a Luxardo cherry**

Preparation

To a cocktail shaker, add the lemon juice, simple syrup, and whiskey and shake with ice for 8 to 10 seconds.

Then strain into a double old fashioned glass over a big rock of Ice.

Add a few dashes of Angostura bitters on top and garnish with the lemon wheel half and Luxardo cherry.

Boston Sour

The Boston Sour is basically just a Whiskey Sour with egg white, which can be confusing today now that most Whiskey Sours have egg white by default. But back in the late 1800s, the Whiskey Sour tended not to have egg white, whereas the Boston Sour must have egg white.

Ingredients

¾ ounce (22 ml)	**Fresh lemon juice**
¾ ounce (22 ml)	**Simple Syrup** (page 28)
2 ounces (60 ml)	**Whiskey**
1	**Egg white**
Garnish	**Angostura bitters**

Preparation

To a cocktail shaker, add the lemon juice, simple syrup, and whiskey along with the egg white and shake dry (without ice) for about 30 seconds to emulsify the egg.

Then add a big rock of ice with a cheater cube and shake again until you can no longer hear the smaller cube in the tin.

Strain into a coupe or cocktail glass and garnish with Angostura bitters.

New York Sour

This iteration of the New York Sour is simply a Whiskey Sour with the addition of red wine. According to Difford's Guide, this drink was known by a slew of names including Chicago Sour, Claret Snap, and Continental Sour, before the name settled to New York Sour in the beginning of the 1900s. The addition of egg white has been credited to more modern bars who possibly started adding it in the early to mid-2000s. You'll notice in old recipes that the drink calls for claret wine, which is a British term referencing Bordeaux wine, so while building this drink, keep in mind that it's best with a Bordeaux or Bordeaux-style wine.

Ingredients

¾ ounce (22 ml)	**Fresh lemon juice**
¾ ounce (22 ml)	**Simple Syrup** (page 28)
2 ounces (60 ml)	**Whiskey**
1	**Egg white**
¼ ounce (7.5 ml)	**Bordeaux-style wine**
Garnish	**None**

Preparation

To a cocktail shaker, add the lemon juice, simple syrup, whiskey, and egg white and shake dry (without ice) for 30 seconds.

Drop in a big rock of ice and small cheater cube and shake until you can no longer hear the smaller cube in the tin.

Double strain into a coupe or cocktail glass.

Pour the wine slowly over the back of a spoon so that it layers on top of the cocktail. When done properly, it should settle above the cocktail but below the foam.

Gimlet

The Gimlet is an old drink that traces its history back to the British Royal Navy and their use of limes to ward off scurvy and make their spirits rations tasty (as I mentioned in the intro to this chapter). Most people don't know that the original Gimlet is a stirred drink instead of the shaken one you'll get in bars if you order it nowadays. And that it was originally made with Rose's Lime Cordial instead of fresh lime. This is because in the latter half of the nineteenth century, Rose's Cordial was the most efficient way to preserve lime juice, and since naval vessels needed something more shelf stable for long voyages, they kept it in stock. In fact, a law passed in 1867 stated that all naval vessels should serve Rose's Cordial to all crews as their daily ration.

When I make the traditional stirred version of this drink, I use lime cordial developed by legendary bartender Jeffery Morgenthaler. He created a cordial that very successfully replicates the flavor and feel of Rose's Lime Cordial with all natural ingredients.

TRADITIONAL

Gimlet

Ingredients

¾ ounce (22 ml)	**Simple Syrup** (page 28)
¾ ounce (22 ml)	**Fresh lime juice**
2 ounces (60 ml)	**Gin**
Garnish	**Lime wheel**

MODERN

Gimlet

Ingredients

½ ounce (15 ml)	**Morgenthaler's Lime Cordial** (page 32)
2 ounces (60 ml)	**Gin**
Garnish	**Lime wheel**

Preparation

For the Traditional version: To a mixing glass, add the simple syrup, lime juice, and gin along with some ice and stir until sufficiently chilled, about 45 seconds.

Then strain into a chilled coupe or cocktail glass.

Garnish with the lime wheel.

For the Modern version: To a cocktail shaker, add the lime cordial and gin along with some ice and shake for 8 to 10 seconds. Strain into a coupe or cocktail glass and garnish with the lime wheel.

Daiquiri

Although the mixture of spirits, lime, and sugar is far older than the Daiquiri, there is something about this drink that makes it stand apart. It is dead simple, just three ingredients, and yet if you mess up any part of this drink, it falls flat. There's a reason why this drink is seen—industry wide—as *the* test used to measure a bartender's skill and experience.

The Daiquiri is credited to an American engineer named Jennings Cox, who was working in the copper mines near Santiago de Cuba, a town near Daiquiri in Cuba. It's said that in 1898, Cox was having a dinner party and making Gin Sours. When he ran out of gin, he turned to what was easily obtainable—rum—and the Daiquiri was born. The first Daiquiri was made with lemons; we know this because the original recipe in Cox's dairy is still around and has been verified. Over time, the drink switched to lime and became a local favorite. Then in 1909, Cox was visited by an American admiral named Lucious Johnson who brought the drink back to Washington, DC.

Ingredients

2 ounces (60 ml)	**Rum**
¾ ounce (22 ml)	**Fresh lime juice**
¾ ounce (22 ml)	**Simple Syrup** (page 28)

Preparation

To a cocktail shaker, add the rum, lime juice, and simple syrup along with some ice and shake for 8 to 10 seconds.

Strain into a coupe or cocktail glass.

Clover Club

The Clover Club was the signature drink of a private men's club founded by prominent members of the journalism community of Philadelphia in 1896. The club, which was originally named the Thursday Club, grew out of a dinner party held by members in 1880. They met regularly at the Bellevue-Stratford Hotel starting in 1909, and as time went on, membership expanded to other prominent members of society such as lawyers, doctors, etc.

Most recipes you'll encounter will omit the dry vermouth, reducing it to a simple gin raspberry Sour, but the better version includes dry vermouth. Although it seems as if the dry vermouth would have difficulty registering in this drink, it is a game changer, creating complexity where there previously wasn't any.

Ingredients

¾ ounce (22 ml)	**Fresh lemon juice**
¾ ounce (22 ml)	**Raspberry Syrup** (page 30)
½ ounce (15 ml)	**Dry vermouth**
1½ ounces (45 ml)	**Gin**
1	**Egg white**
Garnish	**2 fresh raspberries**

Preparation

To a cocktail shaker, add the vermouth and gin along with the egg white and shake dry (without ice) for about 30 seconds to emulsify the egg.

Then, add a big rock of ice with a cheater cube and shake again until you can no longer hear the smaller cube in the tin.

Strain into a coupe or cocktail glass and garnish with the raspberries slid onto a cocktail pick.

Mai Tai

The Mai Tai is the best rum gateway cocktail I've encountered. It was my first experience with this drink that showed me that there were rums outside of Sailor Jerry and Captain Morgan. It is also, not to be too controversial, one of the few perfectly balanced classic Tiki cocktails out there, and I imagine that's why it's persisted for eighty or so years.

The Mai Tai was created in 1944 by Victor "Trader Vic" Bergeron, owner of Bay Area restaurant Trader Vic's. The story goes that one evening, while he was still workshopping the recipe, he tested it on some friends visiting form Tahiti. Apparently after the first sip one of them exclaimed "Mai tai-roa aé," which translates to "Out of this world! The Best!" and so the Mai Tai was born.

This drink was first created with Wray & Nephew 17-year rum, which is now extinct, and many bartenders and cocktail enthusiasts have bent over backward to find ways to recreate the flavor of the original. While I do think these are worthy efforts, I also believe in using readily available and easily replicable ingredients in cocktails, so using a nice aged Jamaican rum or rum blend really sings in this drink.

Ingredients

2 ounces (60 ml)	**Aged Jamaican rum**
¾ ounce (22 ml)	**Orange curacao**
1 ounce (30 ml)	**Fresh lime juice**
½ ounce (15 ml)	**Orgeat** (see page 31)
1 ounce (28 g)	**Crushed or pebble ice**
Garnish	**Mint bouquet** (see page 35) **and dehydrated lime wheel**

Preparation

To a cocktail shaker, add the rum, curacao, lime juice, and orgeat along with the crushed or pebble ice.

Whip shake until the ice is completely melted. Dump contents into a large double old fashioned glass or Mai Tai glass.

Add more pebble or crushed ice to fill the glass plus a bit on top to create a snow cone.

Garnish with the mint bouquet and dehydrated lime.

MU

Bees Knees

Many believe that the Bees Knees is a drink created during prohibition to mask the undesirable taste of bathtub gin, and while that is possible, the exact history is lost to time. Some say that it was bartender Frank Meir who created it in 1921 while running the bar at the Ritz in Paris. Another story has it that it was invented by Margaret Brown, an American socialite and one of the few survivors of the Titanic disaster who spread the drink far and wide on her travels.

Ingredients

2 ounces (60 ml)	**Gin**
¾ ounce (22 ml)	**Honey Syrup** (page 29)
¾ ounce (22 ml)	**Fresh lemon juice**
Garnish	**None**

Preparation

To a cocktail shaker, add the gin, honey syrup, and lemon juice and shake with ice for 8 to 10 seconds.

Strain into a coupe or cocktail glass.

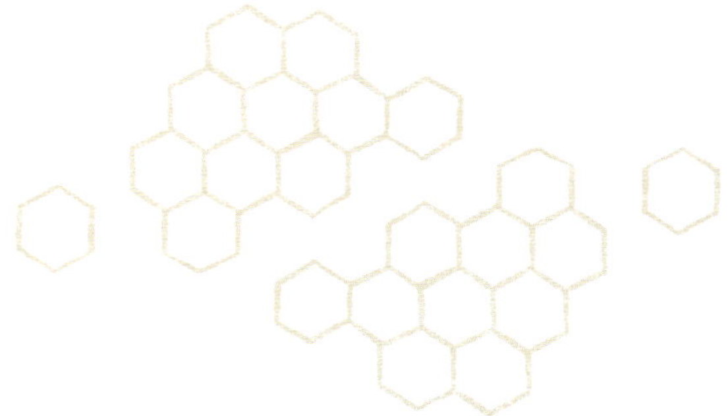

Eastside

The Eastside is the best drink in a bartender's arsenal to convert those who say they hate gin into gin lovers. Of all my years behind the bar, I haven't encountered ONE PERSON who doesn't love this cocktail. I really can't think of anything else in life that garners 100 percent acceptance. This drink is a variation of the classic South Side cocktai —it takes the drink, adds cucumber, and presto chango, you have a nice upgrade. It was created by New York City bartender George Delgado, who made it as a Highball in 2004. It was bartender Christy Pope of Milk & Honey who turned it into a drink served up in a coupe, which is now the most popular version.

Ingredients

8 to 10	**Mint leaves**
3	**Cucumber wheels**
¾ ounce (22 ml)	**Fresh lime juice**
¾ ounce (22 ml)	**Simple Syrup** (page 28)
2 ounces (60 ml)	**Gin**
Garnish	**Small mint leaf**

Preparation

To a cocktail shaker, add the mint leaves and cucumber, and then the lime juice, simple syrup, and gin and press firmly with the muddler without shredding the contents. You want to express the oils from the mint without extracting the green chlorophyll notes while simultaneously giving the cucumber a good firm press.

Shake with a good amount of ice and strain into a chilled coupe or cocktail glass and carefully float the mint leaf on the surface of the cocktail.

Penicillin

The Penicillin was created in the early 2000s by Sam Ross, arguably one of the most famous bartenders to come out of Milk & Honey. He wanted to create a drink that was a riff on the ever-popular Gold Rush cocktail created by T.J. Siegal and decided to use Scotch instead of bourbon. The original uses a honey-ginger syrup developed by Ross, but I've always done it with an equal blend of ginger and honey syrup for efficiency's sake.

Ingredients

¾ ounce (22 ml)	**Fresh lemon juice**
⅜ ounce (11 ml)	**Honey Syrup** (page 29)
⅜ ounce (11 ml)	**Ginger Syrup** (page 30)
2 ounces (60 ml)	**Scotch**
¼ ounce (7.5 ml)	**Peaty Islay Scotch**
Garnish	**Candied ginger**

Preparation

To a cocktail shaker, add the lemon juice, syrups, and Scotch (but not Islay) and shake 8 to 10 seconds.

Double strain into a rocks glass over ice and float the Islay whiskey on top. I find it convenient to put the Islay into an atomizer and spray it over the top of the cocktail to ensure a nice even float and to maximize the aroma.

To garnish, slide 2 pieces of candied ginger onto 2 cocktail skewers and place a skewer on either side of the glass's rim.

Trinidad Sour

The Trinidad Sour always gets a ton of attention because it is usually someone's first time encountering Angostura bitters as a main spirit in a cocktail—which on its face looks like a crazy move destined for failure, but in this drink it works. Bartender Giuseppe González created this drink at the iconic bar Clover Club in New York City, and the drink became an immediate success. Over the years, it has achieved bona fide modern classic status, and almost any bartender versed in cocktails will be able to knock out one of these for you.

Ingredients

¾ ounce (22 ml)	**Fresh lemon juice**
¾ ounce (22 ml)	**Orgeat** (see page 31)
1½ ounces (45 ml)	**Angostura bitters**
½ ounce (15 ml)	**Rye whiskey**
Garnish	**None**

Preparation

To a cocktail shaker, add the lemon juice, orgeat, bitters, and rye and shake 8 to 10 seconds with ice.

Double strain into a coupe or cocktail glass.

Daisy

There are many bartenders and cocktail enthusiasts that put the Daisy into its own category, but for my money, and I've thought *a lot* about this, the Daisy falls squarely in the Sour category. In short, a Daisy is a Sour that often uses a liqueur in place of sugar, but in the past, it did contain a small amount of gum syrup for balance. Many of the historic Daisies that didn't contain sugar, such as the Sidecar and Margarita, have been redone to contain simple syrup, honey, or agave to fill in for the sugar that the liqueur lacks, making a drink that's truly balanced and not overly tart. The original Daisies that we find in Jerry Thomas' *Bon Vivant's Companion* are also closer to the Tom Collins, as they contained seltzer or Apollinaris water, but over time, this drink dropped the fizzy water.

Ingredients

¾ ounce (22 ml)	**Fresh lemon juice**
¾ ounce (22 ml)	**Curacao**
2 ounces (60 ml)	**Gin**
Garnish	**Lemon wheel**

Preparation

To a cocktail shaker, add the lemon juice, curacao, and gin and shake 8 to 10 seconds with plenty of ice.

Strain into a chilled cocktail glass or coupe. Garnish with the lemon wheel.

Margarita

Like so many others in the classic cocktail canon, there are several stories about the creation of the Margarita ranging from between 1936 and 1953. The fact is that nobody really knows how the drink came about, and the answer has been lost to time. It is more likely that, like the Old Fashioned, the Margarita very well could have evolved from the Tequila Daisy. Difford's Guide traced a mention of the Tequila Daisy to a newspaper article from 1936. As we know, Daisies were popular around this time, and the word *margarita* is the Spanish word for "daisy." Makes sense, yeah?

We do know, however, that the popular Tommy's Margarita was first cooked up by San Francisco bartender Julio Bermejo, who was managing Tommy's Restaurant when he created the riff in the 1990s. At the time, agave was new to the market as an alternative sweetener—he decided to take out the orange liqueur and add agave in its place. They started serving it, and it was such a hit, the recipe has persisted to this day.

TRADITIONAL
Margarita

Ingredients

¾ ounce (22 ml)	**Fresh lime juice**
¾ ounce (22 ml)	**Cointreau**
2 ounces (60 ml)	**Tequila blanco**
Garnish	**Lime wheel**

MODERN
Margarita

Ingredients

1 ounce (30 ml)	**Fresh lime juice**
½ ounce (15 ml)	**Agave syrup**
½ ounce (15 ml)	**Orange liqueur**
2 ounces (60 ml)	**Tequila blanco**
Garnish	**Lime wheel**

TOMMY'S
Margarita

Ingredients

1 ounce (30 ml)	**Fresh lime juice**
½ ounce (15 ml)	**Agave syrup**
2 ounces (60 ml)	**Reposado tequila**
Garnish	**Lime wheel**

Preparation

For the Traditional Margarita: To a cocktail shaker, add the lime juice, Cointreau, and tequila blanco with ice and shake 8 to 10 seconds. Double strain into a chilled coupe or cocktail glass. Garnish with the lime wheel.

For the Modern Margarita: To a cocktail shaker, add the lime juice, agave syrup, orange liqueur, and tequila blanco with ice and shake 8 to 10 seconds. Double strain over a large rock or cubed ice in a double old fashioned or rocks glass. Garnish with the lime wheel.

For the Tommy's Margarita: To a cocktail shaker, add the lime juice, agave syrup, and reposado tequila with ice and shake 8 to 10 seconds. Double strain over a large rock or cubed ice in a double old fashioned or rocks glass. Garnish with the lime wheel.

Gold Rush

What's remarkable about this drink, which was created by T.J. Siegal in the early years of Milk & Honey, is that at the time, Siegal was not a bartender—he had come up with the drink one night while sitting down at the bar his childhood friend Sasha Petraske owned. He asked him to make a Bourbon Sour without egg white and with honey syrup instead of simple syrup. And just like that, the drink was born. Petraske named it the Gold Rush and put it on the menu, where it became a hit shortly afterward and is now a modern classic found on menus the world over.

If you'd like to make the original version, use Elijah Craig bourbon. The original used Elijah 12 year, but back in 2016 the distillery decided to drop the age statement and make Elijah Craig Small Batch in its place, a blend of 8- to 12-year-old whiskies.

Ingredients

¾ ounce (22 ml)	**Fresh lemon juice**
¾ ounce (22 ml)	**Honey Syrup** (page 29)
2 ounces (60 ml)	**Bourbon**
Garnish	**None**

Preparation

To a cocktail shaker, add the lemon juice, honey syrup, and bourbon and shake with ice for 8 to 10 seconds.

Double strain into a rocks glass over ice.

Enzoni

This drink has a special place in my heart. Not just because it is a banger of a drink and is super popular these days, but also because I had a hand in helping to create that popularity, which I'm very proud of. This drink was created by bartender Vincenzo Errico while working at Milk & Honey. Errico is an Italian bartender who met Sasha Petraske when he was in London opening the London arm of Milk & Honey. Sasha convinced Errico to come back to New York to work for him and Errico did. Errico went on to create a few drinks that achieved modern classic status, and I believe that the Enzoni is on its way as well. These days, you can find Errico on the island of Ischia off the coast of Naples, tending bar at the fantastic L'ArteFatto, which he co-owns and operates.

Ingredients

4 or 5	**Green grapes**
¾ ounce (22 ml)	**Fresh lemon juice**
½ ounce (15 ml)	**Simple Syrup** (page 28)
1 ounce (30 ml)	**Campari**
1 ounce (30 ml)	**Gin**
Garnish	**2 or 3 grapes**

Preparation

To a cocktail shaker, add the lemon juice, simple syrup, Campari, and gin and muddle the grapes.

Add some ice and shake 8 to 10 seconds until chilled and diluted.

Double strain into a rocks glass over a large rock of ice or cubed ice.

Garnish with 2 or 3 grapes on a cocktail pick.

The Cosmopolitan

This is a version of the Cosmo I'm betting many of you reading this book won't recognize. The Cosmopolitan is one of those drinks that has had several incarnations across the years, but the most popular version was created separately from this one in the 1990s, and that's the one that probably comes to mind when you think of this drink. This version, on the other hand, is much better and more satisfying. Thanks in large part to the complexity of the gin.

Ingredients

¾ ounce (22 ml)	**Fresh lemon juice**
½ ounce (15 ml)	**Raspberry Syrup** (page 30)
½ ounce (15 ml)	**Cointreau or orange curacao**
2 ounces (60 ml)	**Gin**
Garnish	**Orange coin**

Preparation

To a cocktail shaker, add the lemon juice, raspberry syrup, Cointreau, and gin and shake with ice for 8 to 10 seconds until properly chilled and diluted.

Double strain into a chilled cocktail glass or coupe.

Float the orange coin in the drink.

Sidecar

The Sidecar is said to have been invented sometime prior to 1922 by a popular bartender named Pat McGarry at the Buck's Club in London. McGarry is said to have named the drink after the sidecar found on motorcycles of the time. There is some dispute if McGarry actually invented the drink; it is said that Harry McElhone invented the drink at Harry's American Bar in Paris around the same time, but McElhone himself gave credit to McGarry as well. We'll probably never get to the exact truth of it, but either way, the drink was invented sometime between 1919 and 1922.

The original Sidecar was designed to be on the tarter side, and the sugar rim was meant to balance it as the patron drank the cocktail. This doesn't work too well, and in recent years, bartenders have been rebalancing the drink with a little sugar added to the cocktail itself. It's also worth mentioning that the specs are in dispute, and you'll find a wide variety on the internet. I've added two specs below—a traditional and modern spec—which I think are the best representations of the drink.

Traditional

Ingredients

Rim	**Sugar**
1	**Lemon wedge**
½ ounce (15 ml)	**Fresh lemon juice**
1 ounce (30 ml)	**Cointreau**
1½ ounces (45 ml)	**Cognac**
Garnish	**None**

Modern

Ingredients

½ ounce (15 ml)	**Fresh lemon juice**
¼ ounce (7.5 ml)	**Simple Syrup** (page 28)
¾ ounce (22 ml)	**Cointreau**
1½ ounces (45 ml)	**Cognac**
Garnish	**Orange twist**

Preparation

For the Traditional Sidecar, you'll want to prepare the cocktail glass or coupe with a sugar rim: Add a good amount of sugar to a plate, and run a lemon wedge over the surface of the glass making it wet. Roll the glass in the sugar to coat (I like to add sugar to one side of the drink as opposed to directly on the rim). To a cocktail shaker, add the lemon juice, Cointreau, and Cognac and shake 8 to 10 seconds with ice. Double strain into your prepared glass.

For the Modern Sidecar: To a cocktail shaker, add the lemon juice, simple syrup, Cointreau, and Cognac and shake 8 to 10 seconds with ice. Double strain into your prepared glass and garnish with the orange twist.

Corpse Reviver #2

History is murky on this version of the Corpse Reviver, but it was definitely popularized in Harry Craddock's guide, *The Savoy Cocktail Book*, published in 1930.

The Corpse Reviver is one of the few Daisy cocktails that really doesn't need any modern tweaking; its elements are sweet enough that the drink's balance works beautifully in its original equal parts format.

Ingredients

Rinse	**Absinthe**
¾ ounce (22 ml)	**Fresh lemon juice**
¾ ounce (22 ml)	**Cointreau**
¾ ounce (22 ml)	**Cocchi Americano**
¾ ounce (22 ml)	**Gin**
Garnish	**None**

Preparation

When cocktails call for a rinse, I like to put the spirit into a small atomizer, enabling me to spray an even coat of the rinse on the inside of the glass. If you want to skip this step, simply add a small amount of the absinthe (a little less than ¼ ounce) to a coupe or cocktail glass and swirl it around.

Next, to a cocktail shaker, add the lemon juice, Cointreau, Cocchi Americano, and gin and shake with ice for 8 to 10 seconds.

Double strain into your prepared glass.

Paper Plane

The Paper Plane is a modern riff on the Last Word, a drink created in 2007 by New York City bartender Sam Ross for the opening menu of Violet Hour in Chicago. Like many cocktails before it, this one was inspired by a song. Ross was listening to the M.I.A. hit "Paper Planes" (as we all were, if I'm being honest) while working on this drink. The popularity of this cocktail helped to popularize the category of amaro in the United States, which was pretty obscure at the time, and inspired a few well-known bartenders to make their own riffs, some of which became popular in their own right.

Ingredients

¾ ounce (22 ml)	**Fresh lemon juice**
¾ ounce (22 ml)	**Amaro Nonino**
¾ ounce (22 ml)	**Aperol**
¾ ounce (22 ml)	**Bourbon**
Garnish	**None**

Preparation

To a cocktail shaker, add the lemon juice, Amaro Nonio, Aperol, and bourbon and shake with ice for 8 to 10 seconds until properly chilled and diluted.

Double strain into a chilled cocktail glass or coupe.

Aviation

One of the most polarizing cocktails in the canon, the Aviation is loved by some and reviled by many. The drink has not one but two very problematic ingredients—maraschino liqueur and crème de violette—which can come off as overly dry and tasting like Robitussin. There's also an argument over which specs make the best drink and, of course, over the quality of the drink at all. Me? I love a good Aviation, critics be damned!

Ingredients

¾ ounce (22 ml)	**Fresh lemon juice**
⅜ ounce (11 ml)	**Maraschino liqueur**
⅜ ounce (11 ml)	**Crème de violette**
2 ounces (60 ml)	**Gin**
Garnish	**Luxardo cherry**

Preparation

To a cocktail shaker, add the lemon juice, maraschino liqueur, crème de violette, and gin and shake with ice for 8 to 10 seconds until properly chilled and diluted. Double strain into a coupe or cocktail glass and garnish with the cherry. You can opt to put the cherry on a cocktail pick, but I tend to just drop it straight into the glass—that way I have a treat waiting for me when I finish the drink.

Last Word

The Last Word came to prominence in 2005 when Seattle bartender Murray Stenson just happened upon it in Ted Saucier's 1951 cocktail book *Bottoms Up*. So, he put it on the menu at the bar he ran, the Zig Zag Cafe, and it became a massive success. This drink is still very popular in modern cocktail culture, and it's all thanks to Mr. Stenson.

The drink itself was created at the Detroit Athletic Club somewhere around 1915, just before Prohibition. The details are murky, but some say a bartender by the name of Frank Fogarty created the drink, while others say Fogarty was a vaudville performer who loved the drink so much that he spread news of it far and wide. Either way, the drink caught on for a few years and was massively popular until it fell into obscurity, likely due to the onset of Prohibition. Luckily, Ted Saucier was acquainted with it and added it to the book Murray Stenson would find it in.

Ingredients

¾ ounce (22 ml)	**Fresh lime juice**
¾ ounce (22 ml)	**Green Chartreuse**
¾ ounce (22 ml)	**Maraschino liqueur**
¾ ounce (22 ml)	**Gin**
Garnish	**Maraschino cherry**

Preparation

To a cocktail shaker, add the lime juice, Green Chartreuse, maraschino liqueur, and gin and shake with ice for 8 to 10 seconds until properly chilled and diluted.

Double strain into a coupe or cocktail glass and garnish with the cherry.

Ingredients:
Manufactured for
Fever-Tree USA Inc.
New York, NY.
Produced in the UK.
Best Before End:
See base of can.
Store in a cool,
dry place.

CHAPTER 8

The Highball

Like most drinks, the history of the Highball is a bit tough to track down, and that's because it's unlikely there was some flash moment where a bartender seized on an idea to make a new drink. It was, probably, a slow evolution—from people putting water in their drinks to proof them down to then putting sparkling water into their drinks to both proof them down and zhuzh them up. The invention of soda water, also called club soda, can be traced to an English chemist named Joseph Priestly who invented it in 1767. It's a no-brainer that people probably wasted no time adding it to their booze, especially in those days when most spirits were of questionable quality.

The correct ratio for a Highball is technically 2:1, which means twice the amount of mixer to spirits. But I have always maintained (and always will) that this drink is highly customizable to your preference, and you should use that ratio as a guidepost to help you dial in your preference.

The superpower of the Highball is that the mixer dilutes the drink enough to do two essential things: It lessens the ABV of the drink, rendering it about the same strength as a glass of wine, and it spreads out the flavor profile of the cocktail you are drinking, allowing you to taste more nuances of the spirit you're using. My friend Chris Day, who is not only an amazing bartender but also a chemist, put it this way: Imagine the spirit in your glass is people in a room. When you pour a spirit neat, it's like cramming 300 people into a small room. The flavor is super concentrated and so much is going on that it can confuse your palate; it's hard to pick out the more nuanced flavors. But when you add a bit of water or club soda, you lengthen the flavors; it's like taking those same 300 people and spreading them out on a football field. Now it's possible to pick out the guy in blue jeans and a Nirvana shirt, or the blond lady dressed all in red. The more liquid you add, the less concentrated the flavors are, and the more nuance is detectible. The only trick here—and the real art of this drink—is to add enough to lengthen but not enough to over dilute the drink. And so much plays into that, from glass choice to ice to the temperature of the mixer.

Scotch Highball

Credit for the first Highball in America is given to a bartender named Patrick Duffy, who claimed to serve the first one at the Adams House in Boston in 1894. His claim is that a British actor came into his bar and asked for a Scotch and Soda, making Duffy the first person to serve a Highball in the United States. To me, this claim is a little doubtful, and there isn't much evidence to support it other than that Duffy said his claim was supported by the *New York Times*. What is obvious is that Highballs originated in England because artificially made fizzy water originated there in the mid 1700s. As for who brought it to America, who can say? We do, however, know that the first mention of the Highball as it relates to cocktails was in a play that ran in 1894 called *My Friend from India*, and the next year, a cocktail called the Splificator was published in a book called *The Mixicologist* by C.F. Lawlor, which is certainly a Whiskey Highball, although it isn't referred to as a Highball. Then later in 1900, we have an actual entry for a Highball cocktail (spelled as one word for the first time) in *Harry Johnson's Bartender's Manual*.

Highballs can be made with any spirit, and although I thought about adding in at least one recipe for a Gin & Tonic, there really isn't a point. The below ratio is the same for any spirit.

Ingredients

4 ounces (120 ml)	**Club soda, divided**
2 ounces (60 ml)	**Scotch of your choice**
Garnish	**Lemon or lime peel, or lemon or lime wedge or wheel**

Preparation

To the bottom of a chilled highball glass, add a little bit of club soda.

Next, add the Scotch and fill with ice.

Top off the glass with a little more club soda and garnish with lemon or lime.

Rickey

The Rickey is probably the most famous Highball of all time. However, since its inception, society has had a complicated relationship with gin, and thus for many years ditched it for vodka. It is only now coming back to this wonderful spirit. As a result, the Rickey is usually done with vodka or tequila soda with lime, but the original Rickey, which is made with gin, beats them all, in my humble opinion. The story behind the Rickey is that back in the 1880s there was a congressman named Colonel Joe Rickey, who drank at a popular local haunt called Shoomakers. One day, he asked the bartender, a man by the name of George Williamson, to make him a drink with no sugar added and gave him instructions on how the drink should be made and with what. Ta-da! The Rickey was born! According to cocktail writer and bartender Ted Haigh, the first Rickey was made with the colonel's own label rye whiskey, but over time gin replaced the rye, which people liked better, and the drink took off in popularity.

Although, as you well know, I am NOT at all about cocktail traditionalism, the modern version of this drink almost always uses simple syrup. But to use simple syrup is to defeat the original intention of the cocktail. That said, a little simple does wonders for balance, so I leave it up to you.

Ingredients

2 ounces (60 ml)	**Gin** (or spirit of choice)
¾ ounce (22 ml)	**Fresh lime juice**
3 ounces (90 ml)	**Club soda**
Garnish	**Lime wedges**

Preparation

To a highball glass, add the gin and lime juice with about 1 ounce (30 ml) of club soda.

Add some ice and then top off with more club soda.

Garnish with the lime wedges.

Americano

The Americano is one of two drinks, both developed in the 1860s, that directly inspired the creation of the Negroni. The first is the Milano Torino (or Mi-To for short), which is named for the region its two components hail from: Milano, where Campari was born, and Torino, where Italian sweet vermouth is produced. The Americano was developed as a gentle way to introduce Campari to Americans by lengthening the Milano Torino with sparkling water to cut the bracing bitterness of the Campari.

Ingredients

1 ounce (30 ml)	**Club soda**
1 ounce (30 ml)	**Campari**
1 ounce (30 ml)	**Sweet vermouth**
Garnish	**Orange wheel half**

Preparation

To the bottom of a chilled highball glass, add the club soda, Campari, and vermouth.

Next, add ice to offset the volume and top with more club soda as needed.

Garnish with the orange wheel half.

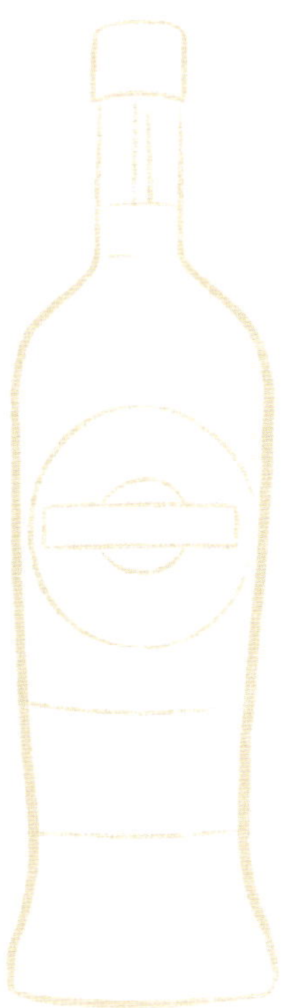

Dark N' Stormy

The Dark N' Stormy is basically a Moscow Mule made with Gosling's Black Seal rum, and if you don't use that specific rum and call it a Dark N' Stormy, you're likely to get sued. The Goslings company trademarked the Dark N' Stormy name back in June of 1991, and they're very serious about it. The history of the drink is hazy at best. Some say it was likely created by fishermen who enjoyed the soothing effects of ginger on the stomach, a cure for seasickness. Others say it was invented in Bermuda where the Gosling brothers created the rum in 1806.

Ingredients

½ ounce (15 ml)	**Fresh lime juice**
4 to 6 ounces (120 to 180 ml)	**Spicy ginger beer**
2 ounces (60 ml)	**Goslings Black Seal rum**
Garnish	**Lime wheel**

Preparation

To a highball glass, add the lime juice and ginger beer and fill with pebble or crushed ice.

Give it a turn or two with a spoon to make sure it's mixed, then top with more ice leaving 1½ inches (3.8 cm) of space at the top.

Next, pour the rum slowly on top of the ice—it should layer nicely.

Garnish with the lime wheel.

Rye Buck

The Buck is one of those drinks that gets confused with a Moscow Mule, but really, the Moscow Mule—which was created in the 1940s—is a copy of the Buck, which has been around since the 1870s. The only real difference between the Mule and Buck is that Bucks are made with ginger ale and Mules are made with ginger beer. That said, the version I like to make has been given the craft cocktail treatment. It's much better to make this drink with fresh ginger syrup and play it up with a little ginger ale, or if you want it a tad less sweet, club soda.

Ingredients

½ ounce (15 ml)	**Fresh lime juice**
¾ ounce (22 ml)	**Ginger Syrup** (page 30)
2 ounces (60 ml)	**Rye whiskey**
4 ounces (120 ml)	**Ginger ale or club soda**
Garnish	**Lime twist**

Preparation

To a cocktail shaker, add the lime juice, ginger syrup, and rye and shake with ice for 8 to 10 seconds.

Pour around 1 ounce (30 ml) of ginger ale into a chilled Collins glass and then double strain the cocktail into the glass.

Add ice and then top off with more ginger ale as needed.

Garnish with the lime twist.

Mojito

There is some evidence that the Mojito dates all the way back to the late 1500s and involved the English privateer Sir Francis Drake. In 1586, Drake dropped anchor just off the coast of Cuba, and it was supposedly on this trip that a drink called El Draque was born. El Draque was a drink made from aguardiente—a crude cane spirit and grandfather to modern day rum—lime, and mint that Drake had on his ship for use as a medicinal herb during long voyages. The drink was primarily used as medicine up through the 1800s until the recipe switched to rum and it was christened the Mojito. The Havana bar La Bodeguita Del Medio lays claim to the modern interpretation of the Mojito, although there are many other theories of how it came about.

There are many big feelings surrounding the topic of how to make a Mojito the "right way." You may be triggered by the lack of club soda in my recipe, but If you really think about what exactly the club soda is doing in the cocktail, I'm confident you'll agree that the drink doesn't need it. And there isn't enough in the drink for the effervescence to read anyway. If you want a sparkling cocktail, I get it—just make a Collins (see page 170) and you'll get all the bubbles you need!

Ingredients

6 to 8	**Mint leaves**
4	**Lime wedges**
1	**Sugar cube**
2 ounces (60 ml)	**Light rum**
½ ounce (15 ml)	**Simple Syrup** (page 28)
About 1 ounce (28 g)	**Crushed or pebble ice**
Garnish	**Mint bouquet** (see page 35)

Preparation

To a cocktail shaker, add the mint leaves and lime wedges; you'll want the mint at the bottom and the lime wedges on top with the peel side facing down.

Add the sugar cube.

Lightly muddle the lime, being careful to only press the mint without shredding it but still crushing up the lime wedges and sugar cube.

Add the rum and simple syrup with the crushed or pebble ice and whip shake (see page 39) until you can no longer hear the ice in the tin, then dump into a chilled Collins glass.

Add ice to the glass, pressing it down with your hand to get as much as you can in there, and make a little snow cap of ice on top.

Slap the mint bouquet to release the oils and scent and then garnish the cocktail.

White Linen

The White Linen was created by Sacramento bartender Rene Dominguez and became very popular at the Shady Lady Saloon. Some bartenders criticize the use of St. Germain as bartender's ketchup; it has the reputation for making everything taste good and erasing mistakes in cocktails that wouldn't work otherwise. Personally, I love the stuff and it's a very nice addition to a refreshing drink, adding a little floral complexity. The fact that it makes everything taste good is a testament to the quality of the product.

As a side note: Be sure to store your St. Germain in the refrigerator to help keep its golden hue longer. Otherwise, it will oxidize and turn brown.

Ingredients

1 ounce (30 ml)	**Club soda**
3	**Cucumber slices**
1 ounce (30 ml)	**Fresh lemon juice**
½ ounce (15 ml)	**Simple Syrup** (page 28)
½ ounce (15 ml)	**St. Germain**
1½ ounces (45 ml)	**Gin**
Garnish	**3 cucumber slices**

Preparation

To a chilled Collins glass, add the club soda.

To a cocktail shaker, add the cucumber, lemon juice, simple syrup, St. Germain, and gin and lightly muddle the cucumber.

Next, shake with ice for 8 to 10 seconds and then double strain the cocktail into the glass.

Add ice and top up with more club soda if necessary.

Garnish with the cucumber slices.

Champagne Cocktail

We have no idea when this cocktail was created. It is as old as when people first started mixing drinks—whenever that was. One of the earliest recipes for this drink can be found in Professor Jerry Thomas's *The Bon Vivant's Companion or How to Mix Drinks*, published in 1862. That recipe, however, is a much different thing than what we do now. The Professor calls for Champagne and sugar to be added to a glass with cracked ice and shaken. This seems to defeat the purpose of a Champagne Cocktail, as the shaking will dissipate the bubbles. These days, we approach this drink a little more sensibly. It isn't the most complex thing on the planet, but it's a nice amuse-bouche (or the drink equivalent of one, anyway) before a meal or at a party before the real drinking begins.

Ingredients

3 to 4 ounces (90 to 120 ml)	**Champagne**
1	**Sugar cube**
3 dashes	**Angostura bitters**
Garnish	**Lemon twist**

Preparation

To a chilled flute, add Champagne almost to the top.

Then, put the sugar cube (do NOT use loose sugar) onto a bar spoon and dash with the bitters.

Drop the sugar into the glass.

Garnish with the lemon twist.

French 75

There is a lot of confusion and misinformation surrounding the French 75. However, what most historians and cocktail nerds can agree on is that it was named after a seventy-five millimeter field gun the French used during World War I. It was first-of-its-kind equipment that could shoot fifteen rounds a minute. The confusion around the drink and its recipe stems from a wholly different cocktail called a "75 Cocktail" that emerged around 1919. Many people equate one with the other, but the earlier drink is so different than the French 75, they are without much doubt unrelated. The first time a drink was published under the name French 75 was in a Book called *Here's How* by Harry McElhone, and that first recipe states that a French 75 is identical to a Tom Collins except that Champagne should be used in place of club soda. It was intended to be served over ice and not as we do it today in a Champagne flute.

Traditional

Ingredients

1 ounce (15 ml)	**Fresh lemon juice**
¾ ounce (22 ml)	**Simple Syrup** (page 28)
1½ ounces (45 ml)	**Gin**
2 ounces (60 ml)	**Champagne**
Garnish	**Lemon peel**

Modern

Ingredients

½ ounce (15 ml)	**Fresh lemon juice**
½ ounce (15 ml)	**Simple Syrup** (page 28)
1 ounce (30 ml)	**Gin**
2 ounces (60 ml)	**Champagne**
Garnish	**Lemon peel**

Preparation

For the Traditional French 75: To a cocktail shaker, add the lemon juice, simple syrup, and gin. Next, add ice and shake 8 to 10 seconds. Strain into a chilled Collins glass over ice and top with the Champagne. Zest the lemon peel over the drink and garnish.

For the Modern French 75: To a cocktail shaker, add the lemon juice, simple syrup, and gin and shake with ice for 8 to 10 seconds. Strain into a chilled Champagne flute, then add the Champagne. Zest the lemon peel over the drink and garnish.

Paloma

The accepted story about the Paloma cocktail is that it was invented by a bartender and bar owner named Don Javier Delgado Corona in the 1950s at his bar La Capilla, which just happens to be the oldest bar in Jalisco, Mexico. But, according to Jim Meehan in his book *Meehan's Bartender's Manual*, Don Javier denied that he had anything to do with the creation of the drink. So, what is the true origin of the Paloma? Nobody knows for sure. Although the drink probably did pop up in Mexico, there is no written evidence of the drink from the 1940s and 1950s to substantiate the history. If the drink was invented in the 1950s, it would have had to be the late '50s—although Squirt, which is the official grapefruit soda to make a Paloma, was invented in 1938, it wasn't imported into Mexico until 1955. When spirits' writer and historian Camper English looked into it, with the help of fellow historian David Wondrich, they couldn't find any mention of the drink in cocktail books of the era. All this is to say that the drink could very well be more modern than we think. Either way, it is fantastic and worth a mix.

Traditional

Ingredients

½ ounce (15 ml)	**Fresh lemon juice**
2 ounces (60 ml)	**Tequila blanco**
1 pinch	**Sea salt**
3 ounces (90 ml)	**Grapefruit soda, divided**
Garnish	**Grapefruit wheel half**

Modern

Ingredients

1 ounce (30 ml)	**Grapefruit juice**
½ ounce (15 ml)	**Fresh lime juice**
¼ ounce (7.5 ml)	**Agave syrup**
1½ ounces (45 ml)	**Tequila blanco**
3 ounces (90 ml)	**Grapefruit soda, divided**
Garnish	**Grapefruit twist**

Preparation

For the Traditional Paloma: To a cocktail shaker, add the lime juice, tequila, and salt and shake with ice for 8 to 10 seconds. Strain into a chilled highball glass. Add approximately 1½ ounces (45 ml) of the grapefruit soda, then add ice. Top off with more grapefruit soda if needed and garnish with the grapefruit wheel half.

For the Modern Paloma: To a cocktail shaker, add the grapefruit and lime juices, agave syrup and tequila. Next, add ice and shake 8 to 10 seconds. Strain into a chilled highball glass. Add approximately 1½ ounces (45 ml) of the grapefruit soda, then add ice. Top off with more grapefruit soda if needed and garnish with the grapefruit twist.

Tom Collins

Nobody knows the exact origins of the Tom Collins, although there is a lot of speculation surrounding its history. From what I could gather, the most credible story is that a bartender named John Collins was serving a popular gin punch at the Limmer's Hotel in London sometime in the mid-1800s. His punch was a riff on a popular punch served at the Garrick Hotel that paired gin with maraschino liqueur and lemon juice. The drink then hopped the pond when a member of the British Royal Artillery taught the recipe to the bartenders at the Clarendon Hotel in New York City around 1850.

There is still some question about what style of gin was used and whether it was called a John Collins or (confusingly) a Tom Collins. Today, if you ask for it in a bar you'll get London Dry gin. But when the drink was first printed in Harry Johnson's *New and Improved Bartender's Manual* in 1882, there are two entries for the drink. The first for a Tom Collins, which uses Old Tom gin, and the second for a John Collins, which uses Holland's gin, a fancy term for a Dutch spirit called genever. By the time the drink appeared in Jerry Thomas's *The Bon Vivant's Guide or How to Mix Drinks* in 1876, it was listed as a Tom Collins. And a Tom Collins it has remained.

I would have written side by side recipes with Old Tom and London Dry, but the specs are exactly the same either way. I highly recommend trying this drink with Old Tom gin, but make sure to get yourself a bottle of Ransom Old Tom, which is lightly barrel aged and adds nice complexity and a little more body to the drink. For light and refreshing, stick to the London Dry.

Ingredients

¾ ounce (22 ml) **Fresh lemon juice**
¾ ounce (22 ml) **Simple Syrup** (page 28)
2 ounces (60 ml) **London Dry gin**
1 ounce (30 ml) **Club soda**
Garnish **Lemon twist and cherry**

Preparation

To a cocktail shaker, add the lemon juice, simple syrup, and gin and shake with ice for 8 to 10 seconds.

Into a chilled Collins glass, add the club soda and then double strain the cocktail into the glass.

Add ice, then top off with more club soda as needed.

Garnish with the lemon twist and cherry.

Airmail

The Airmail is identical to the Modern French 75 (page 168) with a few substitutions. I can say without a doubt that it is one of my favorite cocktails. A perfect drink for early in the night at any celebratory occasion. It was first published around 1930 in a pamphlet put out by the Bacardi company called *Bacardi and Its Many Uses*.

Ingredients

½ ounce (15ml)	**Fresh lime juice**
½ ounce (15 ml)	**Honey Syrup** (page 29)
1 ounce (30 ml)	**Rum of your choice**
2 ounces (60 ml)	**Champagne**
Garnish	**Lime twist**

Preparation

To a cocktail shaker, add the lime juice, honey syrup, and rum and shake with ice for 8 to 10 seconds.

Strain into a chilled Champagne flute, then add the Champagne.

Zest the lime twist over the drink and garnish.

Aperol Spritz

Spritzes in general can be traced back to the early 1800s in the Veneto region of Italy, and Aperol was first introduced in 1919 by Silvio and Luigi Barbieri. But it wasn't until the 1950s that the brothers put it together into a Spritz. It quickly became popular with both the American and European vacationing set, becoming a staple drink during aperitivo hour. Presently, you can find it in bars worldwide. Call for an Aperol Spritz in any bar in the world, and they'll be able to whip up this simple, pleasing drink.

Ingredients

2 ounces (60 ml)	**Aperol**
3 ounces (90 ml)	**Champagne or other sparkling wine**
1 ounce (30 ml)	**Club soda**
Garnish	**1 or 2 orange wheel halves**

Preparation

To a red wine glass, add the Aperol, Champagne, and club soda, then add ice.

Stir lightly to incorporate the ingredients but not enough to dispel the fizz.

Garnish with the orange wheel half(s).

Hugo

The Hugo was created in 2005 by barista Roland Gruber at San Zeno Wine and Cocktail Bar in the town of Naturno, Italy. He was casting about for an alternative to the ubiquitous Aperol Spritz. He decided on a bit of mint combined with elderflower cordial and Prosecco. Nowadays, the Hugo is on every menu in Italy.

Ingredients

½ ounce (15 ml)	**St. Germain or other elderflower liqueur**
3 ounces (90 ml)	**Champagne or other sparkling wine**
1 ounce (30 ml)	**Club soda**
1 or 2	**Sprigs of mint**
Garnish	**None**

Preparation

To a red wine glass, add the St. Germain, Champagne, club soda, and mint and lightly muddle the mint to release its oils.

Then add ice and stir lightly to incorporate the ingredients but not enough to dispel the fizz.

About the Author

Leandro Pari Di Monriva is a longtime Los Angeles area bartender and consultant. Although he began his career behind the bar in 2017, along with producing partner Marius Haugan, he created The Educated Barfly, a YouTube series focused on helping people build better cocktails while teaching them the history and techniques to master the craft. Since then, they have amassed a following across several social platforms exceeding 600,000 followers and have helped mentor thousands of young bartenders just starting their careers. This is Leandro's first book, and he hopes there will be many more.

Acknowledgments

First and foremost, I must thank my producing partner, Marius Haugan, without whom there would be no book. I want to thank my family: Graciela Pari Di Monriva, Maurizio Pari Di Monriva, Natalia Macnamara, Anika Poitier, Joanna Schimkus Poitier, the kids March, Paloma, Connor, Carolina, and last but not least Remy Trahant for always believing in me, pushing me forward, and holding me up when I needed them to.

A massive thank-you to our amazing photographer, David Koung Peng, who shot such beautiful pictures, and Jaclyn Kershek for the next-level prop styling.

I must also thank cocktail writers Robert Simonson, Kara Newman, Camper English, and David Wondrich, who have added immensely to my knowledge of cocktails and the bartenders who make them. A very special thank-you goes to Jeffery Morgenthaler, who contributed to this text and has been a major source of knowledge and inspiration and is always willing to answer a question and help where he can. A special thanks goes to Christopher Day, Garrett Richard, and Sother Teague, who have been staunch supporters and have always pitched in when I needed help. And a big thanks to Brent Falco, who set me on this path in the first place; Kaye Brindley for listening to every tiring word I said and every pitch of the show *ad infinitum* when we first began; and to the whole crew (as well as Regulars) at Cole's French Dip and the Varnish who have always been so massively supportive.

Thank you to all of the bartenders the world over who have created drinks that inspired me—some of which have been included in this book! You are way too numerous to list, but know how grateful I am.

And, lastly, thank you to all of the supporters and fans that I've had the privilege of meeting over the course of the last seven years. Without all of you, this work and this book would not, could not, exist. I would like to thank Darren Orange, Christopher Pinner, Tyler Kroll, Chris Twiggs, Ryland Swearinger, Peter Lee, and Michael Godek for being such huge parts of the success of our show and Discord.

Index